Taxes
for
Humans

PRAISE FOR *TAXES FOR HUMANS*

"An empathetic, spirited, straightforward, judgment-free tax guide for self-employed Americans. Not just a guide to doing your taxes, but a rallying cry for civic engagement. What a gift!"

—William G. Gale,
co-director of the Urban-Brookings Tax Policy Center

"This might just be the most approachable—and dare I say, funny—tax book you'll ever read."

—Farnoosh Torabi,
bestselling author and host of the Webby-winning podcast *So Money*

"If you've ever felt overwhelmed or discouraged by taxes, read this book. I've never felt so seen, supported, and encouraged when it comes to money. Hannah Cole is the go-to expert in the creative community for taxes and bookkeeping, and she has completely transformed how I think about money and taxes over the years. Compassionate, witty, and deeply knowledgeable, Hannah brings a much-needed human approach to a topic most of us avoid. This book is a game-changer."

—Ekaterina Popova,
artist, founder of Create! Magazine, and certified master coach

"Hannah truly understands the unique financial landscape artists, creatives, and freelancers are faced with. She is my go-to expert on all things taxes for the creative community and beyond!"

—Scott Malloy,
senior career advisor at Rhode Island School of Design

"I can't imagine a more approachable book! It's funny, warm, and written in plain language. I want to do my taxes right now!"

—Heather Bhandari,
program director of Foundation for Contemporary Arts, author of
Art/Work, and co-founder of CreativeStudy

"*Taxes for Humans* is more than just a guide for the self-employed – it's a hope machine. Cole transforms every toxic, self-defeating idea you've had about money into self-empowerment through knowledge. She gives you all the tools you need to understand your creative work as a legitimate business, no matter what stage you're in, and the IRS as an entity set up to help you succeed. I never expected to find so many life lessons nestled inside a discussion of the tax code, but that's precisely the promise of this book. Make sure you read it with a notebook in hand."

—Paddy Johnson,
art critic, writer, and founder of VVRkshop

"If you've ever thought, "taxes are confusing," Hannah Cole will walk you through planning, filing, and "oops" moments in the most entertaining book I've read on taxes."

—Joe Saul-Sehy,
creator and host of *The Stacking Benjamins Show*

Hannah Cole

FOUNDER OF SUNLIGHT TAX

Taxes for Humans

A **WORKBOOK** to

Simplify Your Taxes When You're Self-Employed

WILEY

Published by John Wiley & Sons, Inc., Hoboken, New Jersey.
Published simultaneously in Canada.

The manufacturer's authorized representative according to the EU General Product Safety Regulation is Wiley-VCH
GmbH, Boschstr. 12, 69469 Weinheim, Germany, e-mail: Product_Safety@wiley.com.

For general information on our other products and services or for technical support, please contact our Customer
Care Department within the United States at (800) 762-2974, outside the United States at (317) 572-3993 or
fax (317) 572-4002.

Wiley also publishes its books in a variety of electronic formats. Some content that appears in print may not be
available in electronic formats. For more information about Wiley products, visit our web site at www.wiley.com.

Library of Congress Cataloging-in-Publication Data is Available:

ISBN 9781394298891 (Paperback)
ISBN 9781394298907 (ePub)
ISBN 9781394298914 (ePDF)

Cover Design: Wiley
Author Photo: © Nicole McConville

To Mom, whose gentleness shows up everywhere

Contents

Introduction

This workbook is built to help you:

- Work through mindset blocks around money and taxes
- Set up systems to make your taxes easier, every year
- **Do your taxes**

This workbook is a companion to my book, *Taxes for Humans*. The book is where you learn the knowledge, and this workbook sits open beside you as you actually do your taxes. While you can use this workbook without reading the book, it's meant to stay light and actionable, where the book is essential for learning concepts that will empower you and give you peace of mind that you're doing things correctly – including deduction rule specifics; the counterintuitive benefits of your Schedule C (that's the form on your taxes where your self-employment income goes); when, why, and how to pay estimated quarterly taxes; and a whole section on the "oh shit!" tax scenarios so you know how to get out of a jam. Where needed, I'll refer you to the right chapter in the book, using the abbreviation *TFH*. The pair provides a more robust and kind tax education and organizer than you'll find anywhere else.

Who Is the Workbook for?

This workbook is for anyone looking to do their own taxes or improve their tax setup so it's less stressful. It's especially for people who earn income through self-employment. Why? Because that's the hardest part of doing your taxes. By contrast, employees have pretty simple taxes and often don't need help (though you're welcome here, too).

Self-employed people usually have a tax form called the Schedule C, which tracks deductions, calculates taxable profit, and follows some special tax rules. This is often the most confusing part of your taxes.

Is this you? Figure 0.1 shows how to know if you have a Schedule C.

Tax confusion can trigger a sense of dread, stress, and uncertainty about where to start. Without knowing your responsibilities, you can't know when you've met them. You can't relax.

This works great for our capitalist overlords.[1] Anxiety sells. Big tax companies make money when you feel confused, overwhelmed, and powerless. They stoke feelings of fear, stress, and aggravation to sell you the relief – paying them to do it!

There's another option. You *can* do this stuff. I know it because I'm a longtime artist, and I learned how to do it. Frustrated with how hard it was to find clear, practical tax help as a creative, I went back to school for accounting, got my Enrolled Agent's license, and founded Sunlight Tax. (More of my story is in *TFH*.) I've taught many people like you inside my program, Money Bootcamp, where I walk you step-by-step through everything you need to make taxes easier.

You can find all the tools and links I reference in this workbook at www.sunlight tax.com/taxesforhumansworkbook or via this QR code:

✓ Schedule C

- ✓ Self-employment
- ✓ Freelancing
- ✓ 1099 income for contracting
- ✓ Single-member LLC ●
- ✓ Sole Proprietorship
- ✓ Consulting
- ✓ Gig work
- ✓ Side hustle
- ✓ Grant income related to your self-employment
- ✓ Royalty income from self-employment or if you've got an operating oil, gas or mineral interest.
- ✓ Gambling winnings if you're a pro-gambler
- ✓ 2 spouses who equally share a business. ★

● unless you file paperwork with the IRS to be taxed as an S Corp, C Corp or non-profit

★ In which case, mark "qualified joint venture" on the Schedule C. Unless you formed a legal business partnership or elected to be taxed as a partnership, S Corp, or C Corp.

Note: if you're married to someone in this list, and you file jointly, that Schedule C is part of your tax return, too.

∅ Schedule C

Instead, you report the income HERE →

- ∅ Hobby income → Line 8j, Schedule 1
- ∅ Farming → SCHEDULE F
- ∅ Fishing → SCHEDULE F
- ∅ Rental income ○ → SCHEDULE E
- ∅ Royalty income that's not from self-employment or an operating oil, gas, or mineral interest → SCHEDULE E
- ∅ Gambling winnings if you're not a pro-gambler → Line 8c, Schedule 1
- ∅ Scholarship and Fellowship grants → Line r, Schedule 1
- ∅ S Corporation → 1120 S
- ∅ C Corporation → 1120
- ∅ Partnership → 1065
- ∅ Multi-member LLC ★ → 1065 *
- ∅ Non-profit → 990

* But you can elect to be taxed as an S Corp or C Corp instead

○ unless you provide "substantial services" like coaching, or guests' breakfast everyday, in which case, report on a Schedule C

Figure 0.1 Who files a Schedule C?
Source: © Hannah Cole/Sunlight Tax

When you're on top of your taxes, you'll have more bandwidth, empowerment, and focus. Why do I care? Because I believe that your work matters. By shrinking your fear and reducing overwhelm, you can dedicate more time to that glorious work that you do.[2] As a small creative or mission-forward business owner or self-employed person, you're doing empathy-building work that makes our world more connected, representative, humane, accessible, and kind. I believe that when you can focus on your important work, you make the world a better place. That's why I do what I do.

The answer is in your hands: taking the actions in this workbook will shrink the fear monster.

In my experience, when people know how the system works, they feel calmer and more empowered. And they're often surprised to learn the system is more fair than they thought.

Notes

1. Exaggerating. But only slightly.
2. More time for your family, your friends, and your community. AND yourself. Those things matter as much if not more.

Part 1

Mindset: Why Get Good with Money?

You're trying to do something amazing in this world – something much more important than money. You aren't a cutthroat capitalist. So why bother getting good with money?

Here's why: money isn't evil. It's an amplifier. If you're a good person, doing good work, money will help you do more good.

Do you struggle to believe that?

I get it.

List all the words you think of when you hear the word "wealth." How do you describe someone with wealth?:

_____

_____

What do you notice about the words you chose?

_____

_____

_____

Beliefs of Chronic Underearners vs. High-Income Earners

Barbara Stanny's book, *Overcoming Underearning*, studies the traits that "chronic underearners" share. Chronic underearners are those who earn less than their potential, despite their need or desire to do otherwise,[1] valorize poverty, and hold anti-wealth beliefs.

Do you believe you'll become corrupt or unethical if you have more money?

_____

_____

_____

If so, how might that affect the following scenarios?

Negotiating a higher salary _____

Raising your rates with clients _____

Holding boundaries with clients _____

Meeting your goals for financial security _____

Funding your tax-advantaged retirement accounts, like an IRA _____

To build financial security, it helps to believe that you will remain a good person when you have more money. Stay laser-focused on the impact you want to have on the world – *that's* the power you increase when you use the tool of money.

Reflect: how has someone else's wealth helped you? Perhaps they've modeled generosity that shares their riches, spreading joy, care, and opportunity. Could this be you?

Who has helped me on my journey? How has their investment (of money, care, time, attention, resources) helped me?

1. _____

2. _____

3. _____

4. _____

5. _____

Reflecting on that model, what would *you* like to spread in the world?

_____

_____

Another great Barbara Stanny's book, *Secrets of Six-Figure Women: Surprising Strategies to Up Your Earnings and Change Your Life*, outlines seven traits that high-earning women share.[2] Here are my favorite three:

- **Audacity:** Taking calculated risks and stepping outside of one's comfort zone. This isn't about fearlessness. It's knowing that new behaviors can feel uncomfortable, feeling that fear, and doing it anyway.[3]

When have you stretched beyond your comfort zone? How did it feel? What was the result?

_____

_____

- **Profit motive:** Having a clear understanding of one's financial goals and why earning more money is important.[4] That's what we're working on right here, in this section of the workbook. Congratulations! You're doing the thing!

Get Clear on Your "Why"

What is the important work that you do – or want to?

Think big and small, from rest/sick days to changing the world. What's your vision for how doing your work will impact:

- Yourself
- Your loved ones
- Career
- Spiritual/meaning
- Your community
- The world

Example: I want to help _____ do _____, by giving them/doing _____.

- **Financial know-how:** Developing an understanding of personal finances, budgeting, investing, and wealth-building strategies.[5] (We're doing this right now – congrats again!)

When you're willing to get uncomfortable, you try new things. With a clear vision of why getting good with money is important, you've got the necessary motivation. And using this workbook is equipping you with the financial action steps to make it happen.

Fear and Taxes

When it comes to taxes, feelings abound.

Fears can make starting hard. If you're reading this, you've *started*. You've done the hardest part already, so feel good about that!

What are your fears when thinking about taxes?

Notice the fears you described. Are they vague? Specific? Based on confusion or misinformation? Do they stem from a *lack* of something? Control? Knowledge? Money? Time?

Write your observations:

Fear vs. Reality

Let's look at fears compared to facts (Figure 1.1).

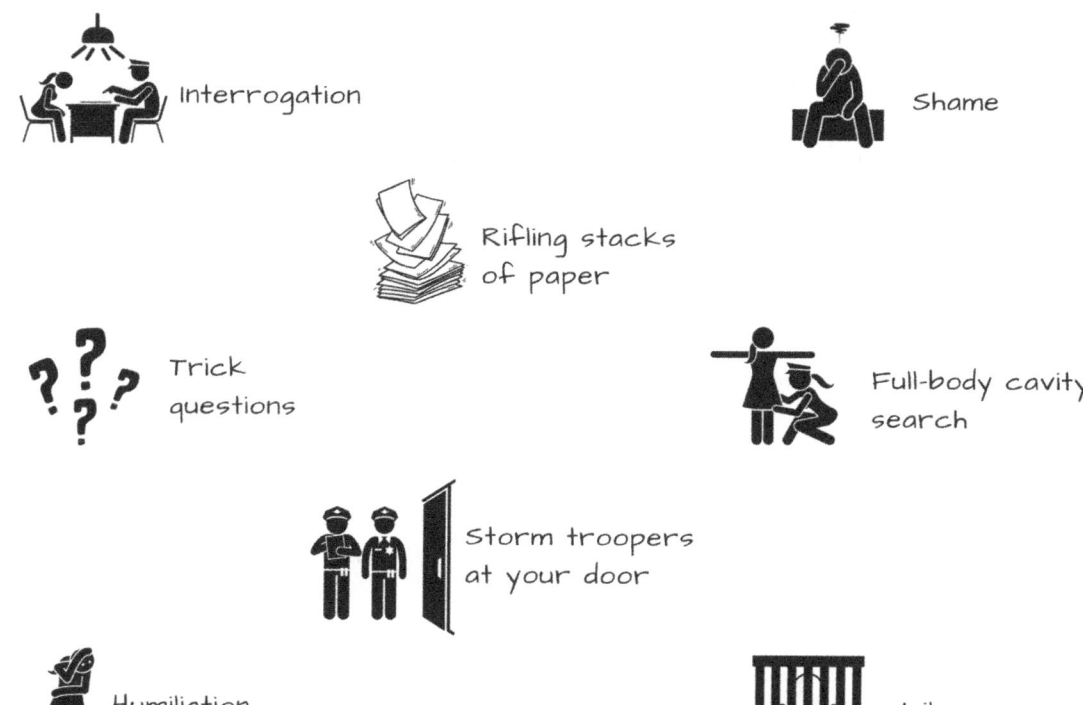

Interrogation

Shame

Rifling stacks of paper

Trick questions

Full-body cavity search

Storm troopers at your door

Humiliation

Jail

Figure 1.1 Word cloud fears.
Source: © Hannah Cole/Sunlight Tax

Here's the truth: some things are a big deal, and others aren't (Figure 1.2).

Big deal vs. not a big deal

Big deal:	Less of a big deal:
• Being on time	• Getting every single deduction (Why? Deductions are optional. If you miss one, you're cheating yourself, not the government)
• Reporting all your taxable income	
• Paying your taxes throughout the year (if you're self-employed, that means paying <u>estimated quarterly taxes</u>. If you are an employee, that means paying through withholding from your paycheck.	• Categorizing every business deduction perfectly
	• Stressing out between two different methods of making a calculation, when the numbers come out a little differently
• Paying your outstanding tax bill by 4/15.	• Making a mistake unintentionally*
• Making a good faith effort to report and pay correctly	• Accidentally transposing numbers
• Filing your annual tax return, on time, even if you can't pay the tax due	

* Don't abuse this. Do your best.

Figure 1.2   A big deal.
Source: © Hannah Cole/Sunlight Tax

Are the facts more forgiving than the disaster scenarios in your head?

Compare your list of fears with the "big deal" stuff in Figure 1.2. Which is scarier?

_____

_____

_____

Your taxes are primarily about paying estimates throughout the year and meeting the deadlines – not perfection.

The IRS knows humans aren't perfect. And taxes are *fixable*, in two ways:

1. You can learn to do taxes better. This will make you feel calmer, more in control, and less anxious, so you can spend more time on. . .literally anything else.

2. Your tax return *itself* is fixable. If you made a mistake, like missing a big deduction, you can file an **amended tax return** (aka a 1040X) to change the tax return you filed (see *TFH* Chapter 16). You can even get money back when you do. (The statute of limitations on that is either three years from the date you filed the return or two years from the date you paid the tax, whichever is later.[6])

Find the Fear-Ending Info

If any of these specific fears plague you, here are helpful chapters in *TFH*:

- A huge tax bill→ estimated quarterly taxes, Chapter 2
- Not knowing if you're profitable, or how much tax you owe→ bookkeeping, Chapter 7
- Not tracking things right→ business deductions, Chapter 4
- Not saving→ tax-advantaged accounts, Chapter 14
- Not able to pay my bill→ payment plans, Chapter 17

- Making a mistake→ amended returns, Chapter 16
- Fear of audit→ TFH is *deeply reassuring* about these. Start with audits, Chapter 19

So remember, your taxes are:

- Fixable
- Learnable
- Improvable

What Do You Want for Your Taxes?

What are your goals when it comes to your taxes?

Think large and small. Do you want to feel more confident or less panicked? Not owe a big tax bill? Know that you've gotten every tax credit or have less tension with your partner over taxes? Maybe you want to get your taxes filed earlier or have cash to contribute to an IRA?

Notes

1. Barbara Stanny, *Overcoming Underearning: A Five-Step Plan to a Richer Life*, (Collins, 2007), 29.
2. Barbara Stanny, *Secrets of Six-Figure Women: Surprising Strategies to Up Your Earnings and Change Your Life* (Harper Business, 2004).
3. Stanny, *Secrets of Six-Figure Women*.
4. Stanny, *Secrets of Six-Figure Women*.
5. Stanny, *Secrets of Six-Figure Women*.
6. Internal Revenue Service, "Time You Can Claim a Credit or Refund," *U.S. Department of the Treasury, Internal Revenue Service*, last modified January 27, 2025, https://www.irs.gov/filing/time-you-can-claim-a-credit-or-refund#:~:text=The%20latest%20date%2C%20by%20law,date%20you%20paid%20the%20tax.

Part 2

The Why of Taxes

Y our tax return's job is to:

- Tally up all your taxable income, including your spouse's income, if you file jointly
- Calculate the exact amount of tax due on that income
- Tally up all the payments you already made toward that tax due
- Calculate the remaining tax to be paid or the overpayment to be refunded

See Figure 2.1.

What does a tax return track?

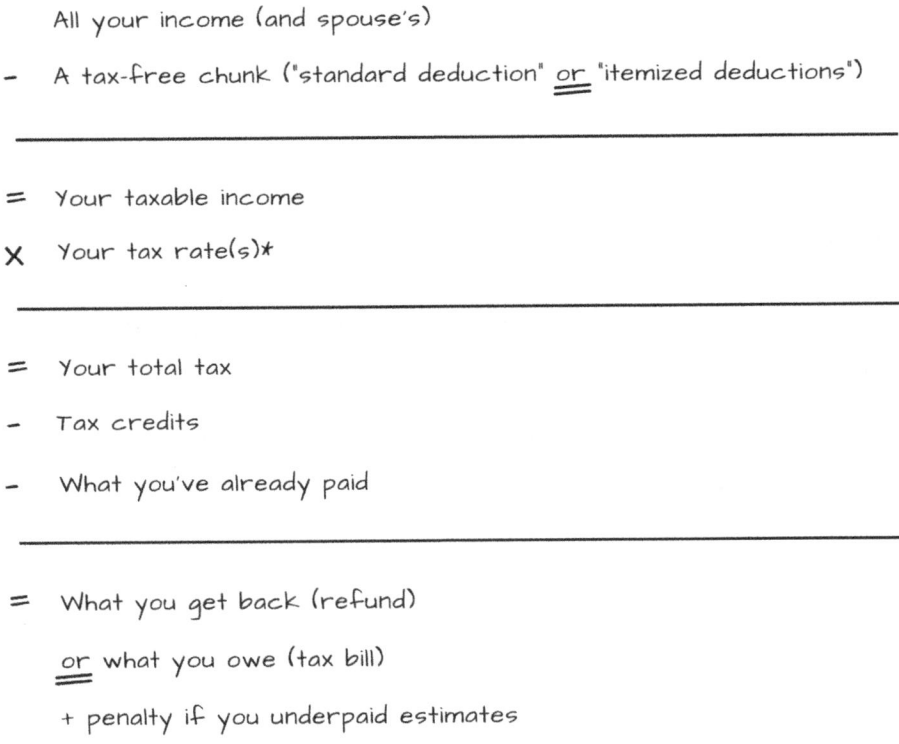

All your income (and spouse's)

−   A tax-free chunk ("standard deduction" or "itemized deductions")

—————————————————————————

=   Your taxable income

X   Your tax rate(s)*

—————————————————————————

=   Your total tax

−   Tax credits

−   What you've already paid

—————————————————————————

=   What you get back (refund)

    or what you owe (tax bill)

    + penalty if you underpaid estimates

* See Taxes for Humans Chapter 2 'How Tax Rates Actually Work'

Figure 2.1   What a tax return tracks.
Source: © Hannah Cole/Sunlight Tax

Figure 2.2 shows the job of taxes.

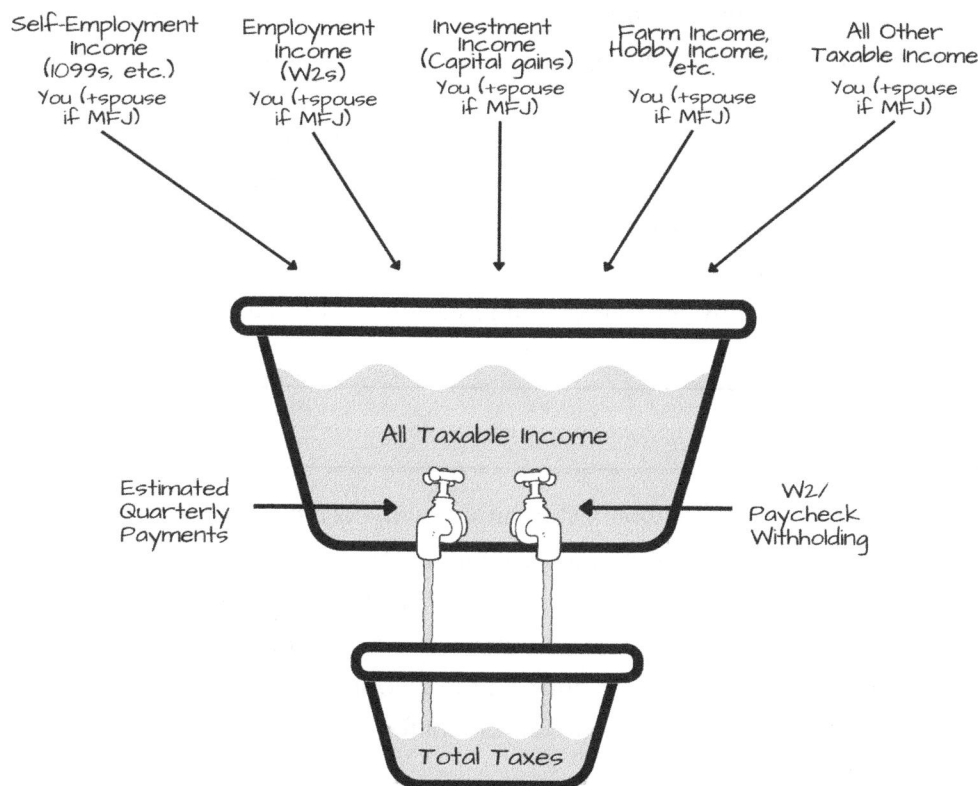

Figure 2.2   Tax buckets.

Source: © Hannah Cole/Sunlight Tax

Your Income

Notice that your income all gets thrown into *one* bucket. People worry that if they have a new business or source of income that their taxes will require a complicated new setup. Generally, no. Just add that new income into the big bucket.

What If You're Married?

Being married *and filing a joint tax return* means you have one income bucket on your tax return, not two – your spouse's income and yours gets pooled together in one bucket.[1] Easy.

You don't have to file jointly when you're married. The other option, Married Filing Separately, means you each file your own tax return, and your buckets – and tax responsibilities – remain separate.[2] Married Filing Jointly allows you more tax credits and potentially lower taxes, but you are also responsible for *everything* on the tax return.[3] For the full skinny on Married Filing Jointly versus Married Filing Separately, see *TFH* Chapter 9.

What's in your income bucket? Write everything down, even the little things. Do you have a job with a W2? Do you have self-employment income, like from a freelance job, a side hustle, or a small business? What about bank interest? Dividends? Investment income? Airbnb or rental income? Royalties? Unemployment? Jury duty pay? Hobby income? Grants?

If you're married filing jointly, include all the income from your spouse. If you don't know their income sources, this is a great moment for a conversation. Go ahead and ask.

_____

_____

How easy or hard was that? _____

_____

Check Your Work

To check your work, review your last 1040 tax return. (If this is your first time filing taxes, you won't have this option). Look at page 1, on the bottom half of the page. This shows a summary of all your sources of income from last year. It's fine if your income differs from last year. But this summary may flag things you forgot to list this time.

Go back and add any you missed.

Your Tax Return Is a Retroactive Tally

Tallying all the income on your tax return is retroactive. Your tax rates are determined by the *actual* total income you earned during a tax year, which you don't know until after that year ends.[4] Taxes get filed after that year has finished when we can answer the question, "What is the total income I made during that tax year?"[5]

You Have to Pay Taxes This Year, Before You Know the Total

In our "pay-as-you-go" system, whether you're self-employed or an employee, you're required to pay taxes throughout the *current* year.[6] In other words, you have to make an educated guess about what taxes you owe, before you know your total yearly income.[7] If you're an employee, you pay through payroll withholding from your paychecks. If you are self-employed (or have income that doesn't have taxes withheld – like rental, farm, royalty, or capital gains income), then you're required to pay throughout the year in the form of estimated quarterly tax payments.[8]

The benefit is that you fill up your "taxes I've already paid" bucket all year long through W2/payroll withholding and/or estimated quarterly taxes. When you do your taxes, this reduces your tax bill – because you've already paid. What relief! No tax bill! Possibly a refund!

Look again at the tax buckets (refer to Figure 2.2).

See the spigots coming out of the taxable income bucket? Those are your payments during the year, filling your tax bucket. If you or your spouse (who you file jointly with) are a W2 employee, then some tax payments come out of a W2 withholding spigot. You might both have this or just one of you.

If you have only nonemployee income, then your only tax prepayment option is the estimated quarterly taxes spigot. In that situation, it's important to pay estimated taxes. Why? If you don't, you're breaking the law (which is motivating, yes?), you could owe penalties, and you'll owe more at tax time. Estimates prevent that.

Notice the tax bucket jumbles all your income together. It doesn't matter which part of your income payments come from. You can use one spigot or two; just keep filling your tax bucket.

Review the income sources list you just made.

What proportion of your income is from sources with withholding? Put a check next to each income source with tax withholding.

In the pie chart in Figure 2.3, draw the estimated proportion of income that has withholding versus not.

Visualize the Percentages of your Income

Example:

Now you try:

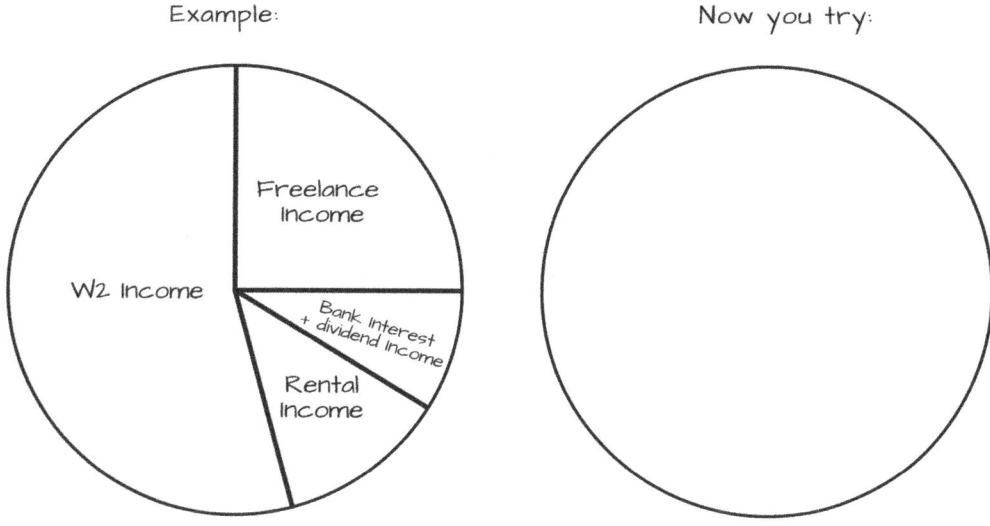

Visualize your withholding
Now shade in the parts that have withholding:

Example:

Now you try:

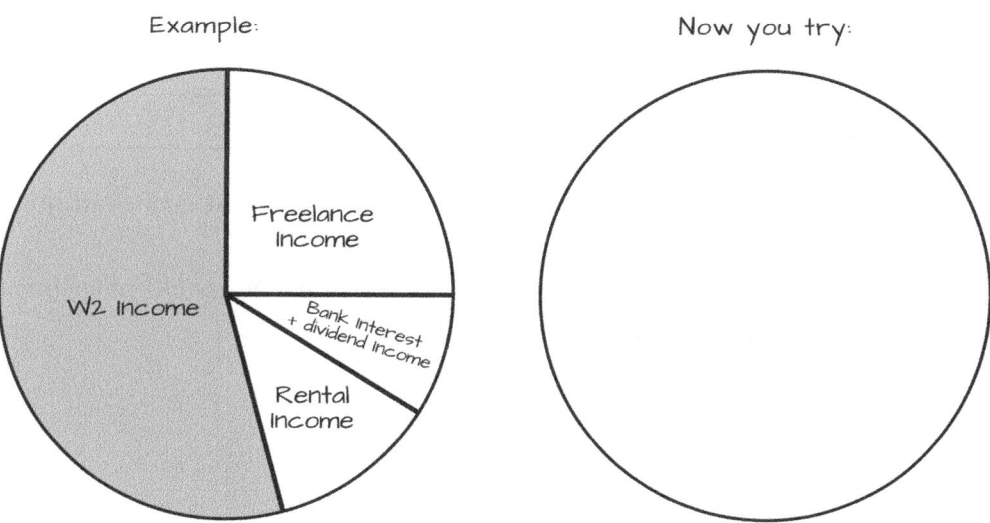

Figure 2.3 Withholding pie chart.
Source: © Hannah Cole/Sunlight Tax

Look at the nonshaded (no withholding) sources of income.

Are you paying enough tax during the year to cover what you owe?

_____

_____

Look at page 2 of your last 1040 tax return. Lines 25–33 list all the tax payments you made before the last tax deadline. What's the total amount of your payments (line 33)?

_____

_____

Compare that to the tax you owed to see how close your payments were. Look at line 24, total tax: _____

A gap between these numbers is normal, but the goal is to get them as close as you can by paying enough during the year in combined withholding plus estimated quarterly taxes. How big was the difference for you last year?

(Line 33 shows if you overpaid; line 37 shows if you underpaid.)

Line 33 overpayment: _____

Line 37 underpayment _____

Especially if you had a substantial underpayment, read about estimated quarterly taxes in *TFH* Chapter 2. It will help.

Might your income this year differ from previous years? What life milestones are you expecting that could cause fluctuations?:

What unexpected events might change your income?

Key Takeaways

- Everyone pays taxes as they go, throughout the year.

- These are estimates based on what you think you'll earn for the year, often based (for simplicity) on what you earned last year.

- The job of the annual tax return is to settle up, or *reconcile*, where you tally the exact amount you earned and what you already paid in estimates and compare it to what you actually owe.

- Imperfection is built into this system.

- Making adjustments as you go is a good idea, because life circumstances change.

- When life changes alter your income, being proactive helps you prevent having to pay a huge tax bill on April 15 and avoids prepayments that are higher than you can afford when your income drops.

Practical Shift: Taxes Are Retroactive

Start now.

You're probably reading this workbook because your taxes feel messy or stressful. Good news! You can change that. Part of what can feel stressful is going back through a year's worth of records that were gathered haphazardly.

Where were you last year, what were your documents, and how did that feel?

Last year's tax information:

Where did you gather it from (bank statements? Receipts? The mail? Email? Looking stuff up online?). Write down what you remember:

How did it feel? Were there parts that felt stressful? Organized? Was any information hard to find? Why?

Write your reflections here.

What can you do differently this year?

_____

_____

What steps can you take to make those changes? (Is it about gathering information? Making decisions? Systems?)

_____

_____

_____

Good news: you can improve your systems, educate yourself, and make better decisions. Bad news: you can't go back in time.

Make Your Taxes Easy: Start Systems Now

Alleviate some of your stress by educating yourself about how your taxes work. _Taxes for Humans_ was written to help you feel calmer and more in control – please read it!

Creating better systems will make your taxes feel easier every single year. It is 100% possible. But since going back in time isn't possible, you can only start systems for your taxes _going forward_.

It's worth it. Future you will be *so* grateful to present you. Your instant-gratification self won't feel the benefits until you're doing this year's taxes. . .which happens next year. The impatient part of you might be screaming at that. But *that's* the part of you that is keeping you stuck in the mess, because you're not taking time now to fix it.

We All Make Money Mistakes

Everyone makes mistakes with money. That makes you human. What's important is what you *learn* from your worst money mistakes.

What kinds of words do you use when you talk to yourself about money? If someone asks if you're good with money, what's your answer?

You're not broken, you're learning.

Practice treating yourself with the ultimate compassion. Write a few sentences to yourself expressing gentle understanding for why you made those past mistakes. What did you learn? Can you forgive yourself? Say so. You might need to hear it.

Your Transactions Happen Every Day

Starting simple systems *now* will make your future taxes easy and eliminates the need to keep "fixing" last year's taxes.

Self-employment income and expenses don't stop and start when you "decide" you're ready and have all your ducks in a row. They keep accumulating – every business transaction[9] will eventually need to find a home on your tax return.

Ideally, these transactions happen in one dedicated business bank account. Preferably, you have a sense of which basic revenue and expense categories they go into. With good software-based bookkeeping set up, you can even automate sorting these transactions.

What does it look like when you've accumulated a year of unsorted transactions and the tax deadline looms?

Draw a picture of (or make a funny title for) the thing that results from trying to look back and organize a year of unsorted transactions:

Right. It's a big ol' mess (Figure 2.4).

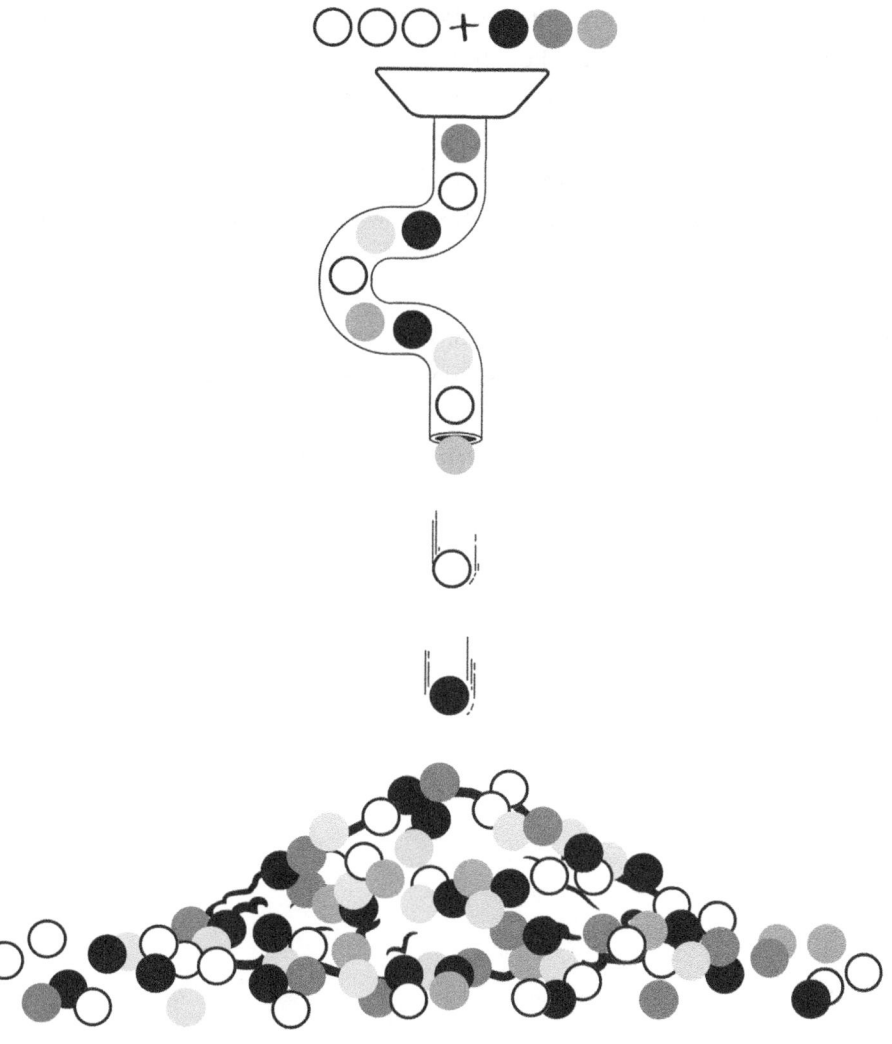

Personal and business transactions

No home = A big ol' mess

Figure 2.4 Personal and business transactions.
Source: © Hannah Cole/Sunlight Tax

Are you ready to start now? On the other side is easier taxes every single year.

Notes

1. U.S. Department of the Treasury, Internal Revenue Service. *Dependents, Standard Deduction, and Filing Information.* 2024, Pub. 501, Washington, DC, 6.

2. *Dependents, Standard Deduction, and Filing Information*, Pub. 501, 7.

3. Ibid.

4. "Federal income tax rates and brackets," *U.S. Department of the Treasury, Internal Revenue Service*, last modified February 13, 2025, https://www.irs.gov/filing/federal-income-tax-rates-and-brackets.

5. Ibid.

6. "Definition of Adjusted Gross Income," *U.S. Department of the Treasury, Internal Revenue Service*, last modified May 5, 2025, https://www.irs.gov/filing/federal-income-tax-rates-and-brackets.

7. "Estimated taxes," *U.S. Department of the Treasury, Internal Revenue Service*, last modified May 15, 2025, https://www.irs.gov/businesses/small-businesses-self-employed/estimated-taxes.

8. Ibid.

9. Approximately. There are a few exceptions.

Part 3

Three Essential Systems

Part 2

Three Essential Systems

Here's where we transform your proverbial "shoebox" of tax receipts into a bento box, with a neat place for everything (see Figure 3.1). This is where we travel from where you are now to where you want to be.

Shoe Box   Bento Box

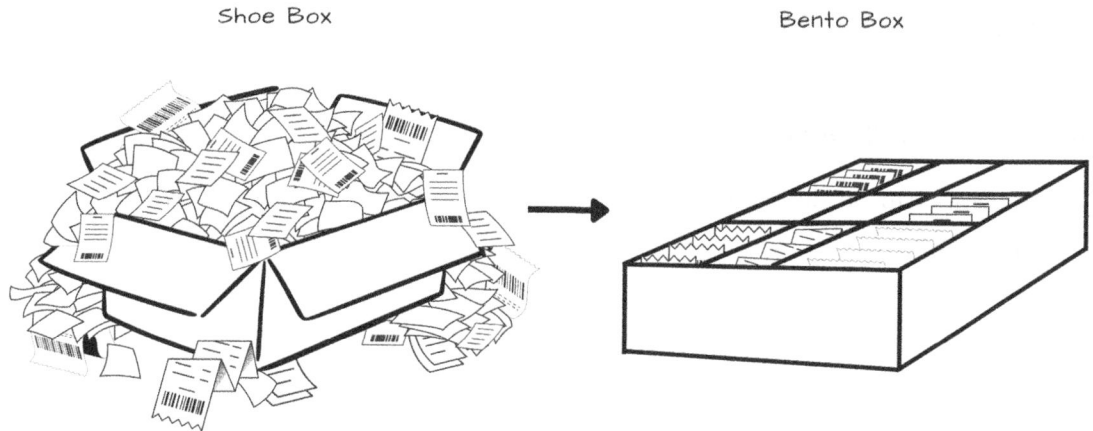

Figure 3.1   Transforming your shoebox into a bento box.
Source: © Hannah Cole/Sunlight Tax

Tackling the Three Main Tax Organization Systems

Let's tackle the three key systems of your tax organization:

- Receipts
- Tax documents
- Bookkeeping

These three systems serve separate purposes. For the full skinny, see *TFH* Part 3.

Receipts

What are receipts for? They serve as proof that the expenses listed on your tax return really happened. Store them for seven years, since the IRS can ask to see them for up to six years.[1] You need them. But don't *do your taxes* from them. Instead, do your taxes from the information gathered in your bookkeeping and your tax documents.[2] Those are the only two systems you need at tax time.

With a separate business bank account and simple bookkeeping, you create a record of each transaction *in your bookkeeping*.[3] So each receipt is noted in your books – and your actual receipts stay in cold storage. It's also why giving your accountant a shoebox of receipts gets you nasty looks. Doing taxes from your receipts (rather than from your books) is stressful. Let's quit that now.

Organize Your Receipts

Your receipts can be digital and physical (paper).[4] Figure 3.2 shows how to organize the paper ones.

How to organize your <u>paper receipts</u>:

- Put each new receipt in your wallet, always in the front. This way, with no sorting, they remain in chronological order from newest to oldest.

- When your wallet is full, put these receipts into a file folder, marked with the current year, in the front. This will maintain the chronological order.

- In January, create a new physical receipt folder for that year.

Figure 3.2 How to organize paper receipts.
Source: © Hannah Cole/Sunlight Tax

Keep your receipts filed by year, because audits happen by year.[5] If the IRS asks to see every travel and meal receipt for 2024, you'll be grateful those aren't mixed in with 2023, 2025, and 2026.

TFH covers how audits happen, what the IRS looks for, and how to keep your records for every business expense including those with extra-stringent rules (like your home office, business mileage, business meals, and travel). The path to confidence in any audit is to educate yourself on keeping all those records the way the IRS requires, since an audit's job is to check that you did. *TFH* Chapter 4 covers business deductions. Consider reading it an act of stress reduction.

How to Organize Digital Receipts

Digital receipts are indeed receipts, typically in email format. If you purchase a business reference book on Amazon, for example, the email confirmation includes your receipt.

Figure 3.3 shows how to organize your digital receipts.

How to organize your <u>digital receipts</u>:

- Create a file in your inbox for receipts by year ("receipts [current year]").

- When you get an emailed receipt, put it into that folder.

- In January, create a new digital receipt folder for that year. (Your task right now is to set a calendar reminder for yourself to do this on January 1.)

Figure 3.3 How to organize digital receipts.
Source: © Hannah Cole/Sunlight Tax

Tax Documents

Next, organize your tax documents. This is not a year-round task since taxes are retroactive – it's something for January that may trickle into February and March (occasionally a stray tax document arrives months later – you'll be grateful to have a place to put it!).[6]

Physical Tax Documents

Pick one place to store tax documents, and every time you get one, without fail, put it there. This can be a file folder (wisely right next to your receipts folder?), a desk drawer, or your sock drawer. Just be 100% consistent when you receive tax document mail to actually put it in your designated spot.

Task: Pick that spot right now. If you need, set a reminder for January 1 about where that spot is, since your documents will start soon after.

Electronic Tax Documents

More and more tax documents will be sent to you over email rather than snail mail. That's cool. Do the same thing you do with your electronic receipts and create a folder for your tax documents, by year. Note that because taxes are retroactive, the tax documents you receive in January of 2029 are for tax year 2028.[7]

Take a minute and create the file folder in your inbox. Label it "[last year] tax documents."

Bookkeeping

The system that takes time and effort is bookkeeping. Bookkeeping is the bento box, capturing every transaction that happens in your self-employment/business into a tidy category. When you do your taxes, you work from this.

Your goal is to turn every transaction from your business into an entry in your bookkeeping. You are laying out the buckets into which each business transaction will fall. The benefit of a good bookkeeping setup (even when it's simple) is that your receipts stay in deep storage (aka ignore them), and you do your taxes from a tidy record of all the transactions, already sorted (see Figure 3.4).

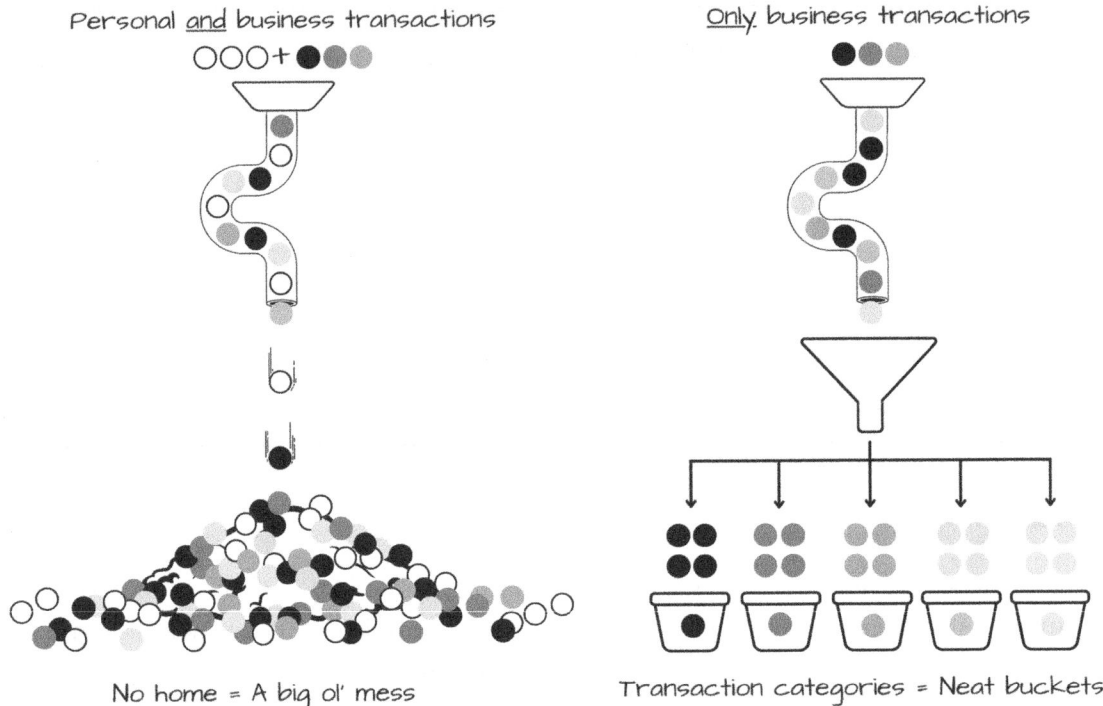

Figure 3.4 Every business transaction needs a home.
Source: © Hannah Cole/Sunlight Tax

Your tasks for bookkeeping:

- Open a separate bank account for your self-employment business.
  - Deposit all your self-employed earnings into it.
  - Pay for all your business expenses out of it.

The magic? Your business account is now automatically recording every transaction that you make. You can review your bank statement and see what happened. If you use this account only for your business income and expenses, it's all there.

Note: your separate account will be used for your business, but it can be a "personal account" offered by your bank, if you treat it as your business account. Some banks only allow LLCs to hold "business" accounts, but that doesn't change the *IRS's* definition of a business (which is that you have a **profit motive**).[8] If you have a profit motive, your business still counts as a business.[9]

Decide which type of bookkeeping is right for you: spreadsheet versus software (see Figure 3.5).

Which bookkeeping is right for you?

Spreadsheet is good for:

- Fewer transactions, manual entry won't be overwhelming

- Side hustle or gig work

- Very part-time or simple

- Your business is small + not growing much/quickly

- Just have a few 1099s

- Just need to track expenses, calculate profit + pay quarterly taxes

- Don't have enough profit to warrant monthly fee for software

Software is good for:

- More transactions, need some automation

- Need to run reports, like a Profit + Loss statement, or Balance Sheet

- Are growing your business and expect more transactions /complexity

- Want to track equity/owner's draws

- Want to connect to your bank account/an automated bank feed.

- Want to analyze your finances each month by looking at financial statements

- Are prepared to pay a monthly software fee + get setup help

Figure 3.5 Which type of bookkeeping is right for you?
Source: © Hannah Cole/Sunlight Tax

TFH Chapter 7 teaches you how to set up bookkeeping. It's the heaviest lift of the three tax systems. It's also the dashboard of your business giving you the most power, insight, and control – it's worth your effort.

Now that you've opened a separate bank account to record your business transactions and you've decided whether to use a simple spreadsheet or software, you're ready to set up categories (the buckets) and start filling them.

Here are two tools to help you:

1. A free visual guide to your tax deductions that shows you what categories you probably are using in your business and how they translate to the tax category. Go to www.sunlighttax.com/deductionsguide.

2. If you want a spreadsheet bookkeeping system and you want my premade spreadsheet with expense categories set up already (plus bonus calculation formulas and tips for the harder categories like home office, travel, and meals), go to www.sunlighttax.com/taxesforhumans.

Feeling resistance to
your numbers? Try out
this thought: book-
keeping is self-care.

Are you feeling resistance? Name it here. Are you scared to look at your numbers, because they might show you a situation you don't like? Do your numbers make you feel judged? Do you just feel busy and overwhelmed, and it feels like a lot of work? Get clear on *what* the resistance is.

My resistance to tracking my numbers as a hard-working but low-paid artist was that they made visible a story that I didn't want to see. They whispered, "All the time away from your partner, working hard on this career that people doubted in the first place, is eating away at your relationship. The prestige does nothing to pay your rent. Maybe the doubters were right."

My numbers used to make me feel awful. My disorganization caused me stress, and not knowing my numbers enabled me to avoid the truth. That hurt me in other ways (tax time fights over my disorganization, embarrassment at living up to the "starving artist" stereotype, and intense money anxiety). Ultimately, I decided that the truth existed whether or not I set up better systems. But systems *would* eliminate some of my other problems (like tax fights and the anxiety of not knowing how much money I was making or owed). I felt the fear and did it anyway, and I stand before you now as someone who takes comfort in my numbers.

Be Dalai Lama–level kind to yourself.

My advice to that version of myself?

Your numbers are what they are. It may feel hard to look at them, but when you do, you can feel less anxiety, make your taxes easier, and evaluate potential changes.

OG feminist Gloria Steinem famously said something that came true for me: "The truth will set you free. But first it will piss you off.[10]"

Make It Fun

If bookkeeping feels hard to you, you're normal. Think about how to make it pleasant.

Neuroscience shows that creating positive associations with a new habit helps make it stick.[11]

Exercise: Brainstorm all the ways to create a calm, kind environment for yourself to set up your bookkeeping (and then every time you do your books). Maybe cleaning your desk, lighting a candle, sending the kids out of the house, playing music, drinking a cappuccino or hazy IPA?

Starting is the hardest part – for me at least. Once I sit down with my bank statements and get involved in the task, it isn't so bad.

Starting is a major victory. Plan a reward.

What's your low-bar goal for starting? Is it opening your bank app and looking at your business bank statements? Opening your bookkeeping spreadsheet?

_____

_____

What is your reward for meeting that goal? Meet a friend to debrief or have a small treat?

_____

_____

Plan When You'll Do Your Bookkeeping

Now, think about how frequently you need to do your bookkeeping. Break this into two parts: setup and ongoing maintenance.

Plan Your Bookkeeping Setup

Your setup may take a few hours to a day to complete. Consider breaking that into sessions.

Task: Think of how many transactions you have in your self-employed business (low to high), and decide how much time setting up your books will take. Consider three hours on the low side, up to a full day on the higher end, if you're setting up on a spreadsheet.

List the guesstimated number of hours here:

_____

_____

You know yourself. Do you have a deep-focus brain that wants long stretches of uninterrupted time? Do you get impatient quickly and do better with shorter sessions?

- Task: Schedule the hours on your calendar in the next month when you will set up your bookkeeping.

Using Software?

If you're planning to use bookkeeping software, hire a professional bookkeeper to do the setup. I explain "why" in detail in *TFH* Chapter 7, but the upshot is that it requires technical training. It's cheaper to hire a pro at the outset than to fix compounded mistakes from badly set up bookkeeping software.

That said, you'll have prep tasks to find and engage a bookkeeper and then to deliver them the information they need. This also takes time.

Plot these out here, using this template:

- How will I locate a good bookkeeper? Which friends and professionals can I ask for a referral? Name names! _____

- When will I do that? _____

  Now write it in your calendar.

- The rest comes after you engage the bookkeeper, on their timeline. Be aware that you'll need to learn their system, deliver them your information, grant them read-only access to your statements, and possibly open a new bank account. Put these upcoming tasks on your radar.

Plan Your Regular Bookkeeping (Ongoing Maintenance)

Whether you use a spreadsheet or software, you have to schedule regular time to do your bookkeeping. Depending on how complex your business is, you might be able to do this just once or twice a year (only those who don't/won't owe estimated quarterly taxes should consider this), every quarter (especially right before the estimated tax deadlines), or every month.

What bookkeeping frequency feels right for you at this stage? (You can change this later): _____

With your three systems in place, every transaction is recorded and sorted into buckets that transfer directly to your tax return categories. Even if you don't do regular bookkeeping, these steps will help you organize your information at tax time.

Feel the ease. And get yourself a little something to celebrate.

Put It into Practice

Each quarter:

- Do your bookkeeping.
- Pay your *federal* estimated taxes.
- Pay your *state* estimated taxes.

These are the estimated quarterly tax deadlines:

- April 15
- June 15
- September 15
- January 15[12]

By giving yourself plenty of time to meet those deadlines, you can do your bookkeeping without panic. Ideally you'll grab your bank statements and start categorizing those expenses and tracking that income a few days after the start of the month, when your statement becomes available. So a good calendar reminder to set for yourself may be:

- April 3
- June 3
- September 3
- January 3

Task: If you will be paying estimated quarterly taxes, then I suggest these dates. If you will be doing your books monthly, select calendar dates in between those quarterly ones. Based on your bookkeeping frequency, calendar all of the dates you need to remember – now.

Each year, in January, complete the checklist shown in Figure 3.6.

Your January Checklist

Each year, in January:

☐ Set up your receipts' folder (in your inbox, and in a physical file folder).

☐ Set up your tax document retention place (sock drawer, file folder, etc) for this year.

☐ Bonus January task: Note your odometer for your "ending mileage" for last year's taxes. This same number is your "beginning mileage" for the coming year's taxes.

☐ Bonus January task: While you're at it, snap pics of your home office, which demonstrates that it's used exclusively for your business... (with no personal stuff like a guest bed or your dining room table). These photos go in the storage files, in your physical tax files for this year, or in your inbox tax files.

Figure 3.6 January checklist.
Source: © Hannah Cole/Sunlight Tax

Notes

1. "How long should I keep records?," *U.S. Department of the Treasury, Internal Revenue Service*, last modified August 20, 2024, https://www.irs.gov/businesses/small-businesses-self-employed/how-long-should-i-keep-records#:~:text=Period%20of%20limitations%20that%20apply%20to%20income%20tax%20returns&text=Keep%20records%20for%207%20years,income%20shown%20on%20your%20return.

2. "Gather your documents," *U.S. Department of the Treasury, Internal Revenue Service*, last modified June 25, 2025, https://www.irs.gov/filing/gather-your-documents.

3. "What kind of records should I keep," *U.S. Department of the Treasury, Internal Revenue Service*, last modified February 28, 2025, https://www.irs.gov/businesses/small-businesses-self-employed/what-kind-of-records-should-i-keep.

4. Ibid.

5. "IRS audits," *U.S. Department of the Treasury, Internal Revenue Service*, last modified September 9, 2024, https://www.irs.gov/businesses/small-businesses-self-employed/irs-audits.

6. "Amdt 5.4.7.2.2 Retroactive Taxes," *U.S. Constitution Annotated*, https://www.law.cornell.edu/constitution-conan/amendment-5/retroactive-taxes.

7. "Amdt 5.4.7.2.2 Retroactive Taxes."

8. Sandra Feldman, "Profit motive required to claim business deductions," *Wolters Kluwer*, last modified January 22, 2022, https://www.wolterskluwer.com/en/expert-insights/profit-motive-required-to-claim-business-deductions#:~:text=The%20nine%2Dfactor%20test%20to%20determine%20profit%20motive&text=Among%20the%20factors%20the%20IRS,the%20income%20for%20your%20livelihood.

9. Ibid.

10. In my case, it pissed me off about the art world, and its exploitative use of "prestige" and "exposure" in lieu of real payment. I still have some very salty feelings. See Gloria Steinem, *The Truth Will Set You Free, But First It Will Piss You Off!: Thoughts on Life, Love, and Rebellion* (Random House 2020).

11. James Clear, *Atomic Habits: An Easy and Proven Way to Build Good Habits & Break Bad Ones,* (Avery, 2018).

12. Yes, these are not evenly spaced. Good catch if you noticed. You can thank Congress and the Federal fiscal year. But these are still the deadlines. See "When to pay estimated tax," *U.S. Department of the Treasury, Internal Revenue Service*, last modified February 3, 2025, https://www.irs.gov/faqs/estimated-tax/individuals/individuals-2.

Part 4

Doing Your Taxes

Here's the reward for the systems you've put in place. If your new systems captured the full tax year, congratulations! This will feel so much easier.

(If not, it's OK. Go back to Part Three and put those systems into place. Just start now. You can do it.)

Remember, this workbook focuses on the *tasks* of making your taxes easier. The *knowledge* to understand it all (and the relief of knowing you've done enough) is covered in *TFH* Part Four: doing your taxes.

Steps for Doing Your Taxes

To do your taxes, you'll need to:

1. Gather your business income numbers from your books.
2. Complete the questions and the tax documents checklist in the Tax Organizer.

Gather Business Income Numbers from Your Books

The heaviest lift when you're self-employed is completing your prior-year bookkeeping. If you've recorded and sorted every transaction already, you get a gold star. If you haven't, let's make a plan.

Why are we talking bookkeeping *again*, when we talked about it already in the systems section? Because bookkeeping is a year-round task. To do your taxes, you need the full year of total income and total expenses for each deduction category. The more bookkeeping you do during the year, the less you need to do at tax time. Whatever isn't finished is first on your task list, before starting your taxes.

Snapshot: Where on the line is your current bookkeeping (Figure 4.1)?

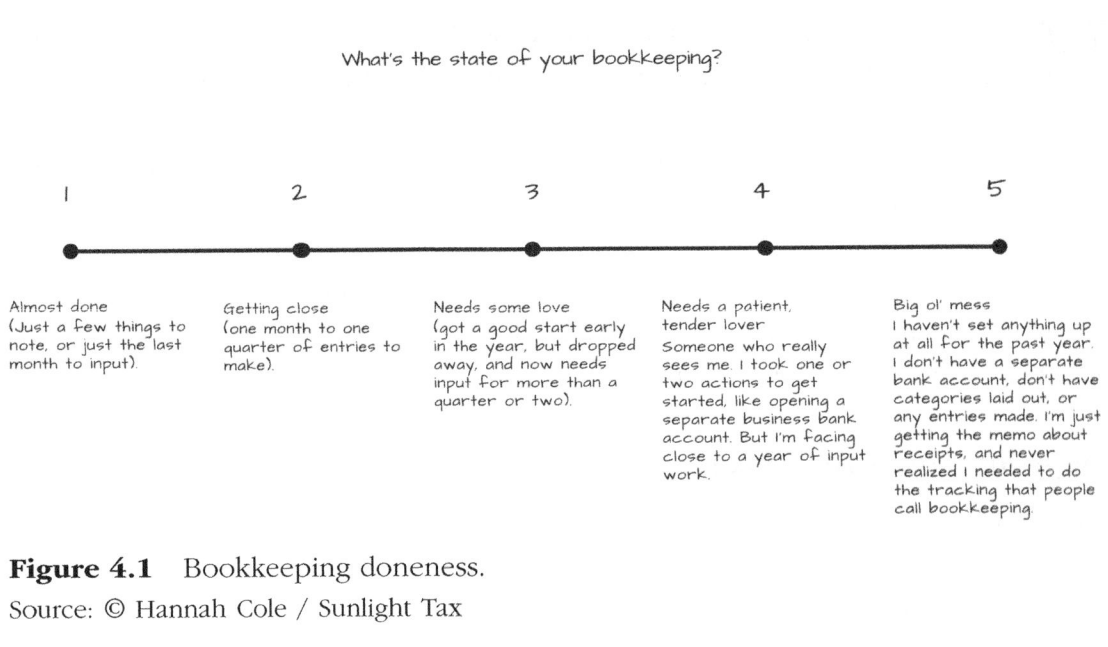

Figure 4.1 Bookkeeping doneness.
Source: © Hannah Cole / Sunlight Tax

What's left for you to do before you know your year-end totals?

_____

_____

Now, calendar the sessions you need to finish your bookkeeping to have your totals ready to do your taxes, and refer to Part Three as needed (or *TFH* Chapter 7).

Then, take a deep breath. You're a lovely human. Your books are not a comment on that. I mean this.

Fixing next year:

Select where on the line you want your numbers to be at this time *next* year to make tax time feel manageable.

Based on that, how can you do *this year's* bookkeeping to make next year's tax time feel easier? What cadence would work best for you (quarterly, monthly)?

_____

_____

_____

You get rewards for finishing your taxes early (see Figure 4.2).

Rewards for finishing your taxes early:

- Tax refunds come faster the earlier you file your tax return

- Accountants may offer early-season discounts (in January and February)

- IRS call wait times are shorter in early season

- Lower stress, more time to make decisions

- Less tension with your partner

- More time to set up an IRA and transfer money

Figure 4.2   Rewards for finishing taxes early.
Source: © Hannah Cole/Sunlight Tax

Next, let's talk about the numbers you need from your books.

When your bookkeeping is done, gather the following:

If your bookkeeping is on software, pull the following (in the "reports" section; plug in these dates):

- A "profit and loss" statement for January 1 to December 31 of the year that just ended
- A "balance sheet" for December 31 of the year that just ended

If your books are on a spreadsheet, you need the following:

- Totals from each expense category
- Total income
- The bookkeeping spreadsheet for reference as you do your taxes

Keep These Lists

As you complete the following tax organizer, use the spaces for each list.

Tax Questions

What comes up as you gather materials? There may be tax credits to research, questions about your situation, etc. Make this list and then look up the answers (*TFH* will answer many of them!). If this gets long, it's time to call a tax professional.

1. _____
2. _____
3. _____
4. _____
5. _____

Decisions to Make

Do you want to contribute to an IRA or other retirement savings account? (Please say yes.) Is this a better year for a Roth or Traditional account?

1. _____
2. _____
3. _____
4. _____
5. _____

Action Items

Note the actions to take, like calling a brokerage to open an IRA or moving money into your bank account in time for the IRS autodraft of your tax payment.

1. _____
2. _____
3. _____
4. _____
5. _____

Upcoming Life/Income Changes That May Require Adjustments for This Year

Assess your current W2 withholding or estimated quarterly tax payments, and determine if you need to increase or decrease them.

1. _____
2. _____
3. _____
4. _____
5. _____

Income Tax Organizer

This organizer will help you gather your tax data so you can complete your taxes or hand everything to your tax preparer. Some questions may seem irrelevant – they are here because the law requires you to answer them. Remember that your signature (and your spouse's if relevant) on your tax return testifies that everything on it is correct, and you have the records and receipts to document what you claim.

No tax organizer is perfect. This one balances the needs of a self-employed person without overwhelming you with unlikely scenarios. However, if you have an outlier scenario, this organizer may not surface every question you need to answer (examples: clergy, airline employees, investors in oil and minerals, and military personnel may need additional info).

This form is a perfect starting point, and 95% of it will stay relevant every year. Be aware that tax law changes can add/subtract a few questions. Before you start each year, do an internet search for "tax changes for [insert tax year]."

For a blank, printable version, go to www.sunlighttax.com/taxesforhumans workbook or use this QR code:

(continued)

Personal Information

	Your Information	Your Spouse's Information
Legal Name [First, MI, Last]		
Social Security Number		
Date of Birth		
Current Address	*(This becomes your address for IRS correspondence until you file a tax return with a different address)*	if different
Email		
Phone		
Occupation *(and short description of it)*		
[the following two questions are if you're working with a tax preparer, for their knowledge, not your tax forms:]		
Preferred Name		
Pronouns		

Do you want to allocate $3 to the Presidential Election Fund?
This doesn't add to your tax due; it just earmarks $3 for public campaign financing of elections.　　　　　　　　　　　　　[YES]　　[NO]

At any time during [relevant tax year] did you: (a) receive (as reward, award, or payment for property or services); or (b) sell, exchange, or otherwise dispose of a digital asset (or a financial interest in a digital asset)?
Think NFTs, crypto, stablecoins, etc.　　　　　　　　　　[YES]　　[NO]

Are you legally blind?　　　　　　　　　　　　　　　　　[YES]　　[NO]

Your Filing Status

This is a key decision for your taxes. For more info, see TFH *Chapter 9.*

☐ [SINGLE]

☐ [MARRIED FILING JOINT]

☐ [MARRIED FILING SEPARATE]

☐ [HEAD OF HOUSEHOLD] *This is for unmarried taxpayers who support a qualifying dependent.*

☐ [QUALIFYING SURVIVING SPOUSE][1]

☐ [NOT SURE] *Add this to your Tax Questions list for research; read* TFH *Chapter 9 or use this great tool at the IRS website to help you:* https://www.irs.gov/help/ita/what-is-my-filing-status.

Driver's License Information

	You	Spouse
State	_____	_____
Issue Date	_____	_____
Expiration Date	_____	_____
License Number	_____	_____
NY only – Document ID number *Here's help finding this NY number:* https://dmv.ny.gov/driver-license/sample-photo-documents	_____	_____

(continued)

Did your spouse die within the last three years?   [YES]   [NO]

Year of death   [Date]

Have you remarried?   [YES]   [NO]

Dependent Information

A dependent can be a child or other qualifying relative. If unsure, see the IRS guidelines at https://www.irs.gov/help/ita/whom-may-i-claim-as-a-dependent.

Do you have any dependents (child or qualifying relative)?   [YES]   [NO]

Fill this out for each of your dependents.

	Name [First, MI, Last]	Social Security Number	Date of Birth	Relationship to Taxpayer (Child, Disabled Parent, etc.)
Dependent 1				
Dependent 2				
Dependent 3				
Dependent 4				
Dependent 5				

If You Moved/Address Change

Are you active duty military, and did you move this year while on active duty?   [YES]   [NO]

Former Address

Date of move _____

Former Address _____

Moving expenses are deductible only for active duty military.[2] However, a move may affect your home office deduction, your mortgage interest, and possibly your number of state income tax returns.

Refund and Payment Information

You probably like receiving a direct deposit but feel nervous about a direct debit, before knowing if you owe money. The IRS cannot withdraw any amount besides what is stated on your 1040 as the amount you owe.[3] They will not take out extra money or past debts. Setting up direct deposit/ direct debit is a great backstop for fallible human memory. See TFH *Chapter 9 for more.*

Do you want your federal refund direct deposited? (If applicable.)
Your refund will arrive as soon as your return is processed.   [YES]   [NO]

Do you want your federal taxes due direct debited? (If applicable.)
Your tax due will be debited on April 15 by default, or the date you request, if you prefer.   [YES]   [NO]

Do you want your first federal estimated quarterly tax payment direct debited? (If applicable.) *You can elect to have your first, or even all, of your estimates direct debited.[4] In my tax practice, I rarely let folks debit all four, because life is too uncertain. If you direct debit your first estimate, make note of your second, third, and fourth payment deadlines (June 15, September 15, and January 15), since those won't happen automatically.*   [YES]   [NO]

Do you want your state refund direct deposited? (If applicable.) *Your refund will arrive as soon as your return is processed.*   [YES]   [NO]

(continued)

Do you want your state taxes due direct debited? (If applicable.) *Your tax due will be debited on April 15 by default, or a date you request.*   [YES]   [NO]

Do you want your first state estimated quarterly tax payment direct debited? *(If your state allows. Some states require debit to be set up with your tax return, and others require separate setup.)*   [YES]   [NO]

Bank Information

Fill out if working with a tax preparer.

Bank Name _____

Type of bank account

- Checking
- Savings

Bank Routing Number _____

Bank Account Number _____

Initial Income Questions

	You	**Spouse**
How many W2 forms did you receive during the tax year?	_____	_____
Approximately how much money did you earn from W2 income (as an employee, *not* from freelance work)?	_____	_____
Did you earn income as a freelancer, contractor, sole proprietor, or single-member LLC? *If you answered "yes," complete the following **Business Income and Expenses Information** section. If you answered "no," move on to the Miscellaneous Income section.*	[YES] [NO]	[YES] [NO]

Business Income and Expenses Information

For any self-employment income, including freelance work, sole proprietorships, or single-member LLCs.

Business 1

If there is more than one business, copy this section as needed, and fill out for each.

DO NOT INCLUDE ANY W2 INCOME/info in this section. W2 income has been taxed, and your business income has not – they must stay separate.

This section identifies all income earned in your freelance/self-employed/small business capacity (i.e., sales of your work, cash sales, client payments, grants, etc.).

For an empowering primer on self-employment, see TFH *Chapters 2 and 3. For business expense specifics, including how to document them legally, see* TFH *Chapter 4.*

Is this your business or your spouse's? • [Mine] • [My Spouse's]	Was this your first year in business? [YES] [NO]
Business Name (if you have one) _____	Business EIN (if you have one) _____

Business Address (if different from your home address) _____

Brief description of the business' principle activity, and product or service

_____

_____

_____

_____

_____

(continued)

Business Income

Add additional lines below as needed:

A. Income Reported on a 1099		B. Income *Not* Reported on a 1099	
*This is income earned in your business that you **did** get a 1099 for.*		*This is income earned in your business that you **didn't** get a 1099 for.*	
Amount:	**Paid by:**	**Amount:**	**Paid by:**
_____	_____	_____	_____
Total Sum on 1099s:		Total Sum not on 1099s:	

Add the total sum from column A (1099s) to the total sum from column B (no 1099s):

_____

Based on your reporting here, this number is **your gross receipts** (i.e., total freelance income).[5]

Is this correct?   [YES]   [NO]

*(This is a critical number, so when you review your taxes before submitting, double-check that your **Schedule C, Part I, line 1** equals this number. If not, check to see if you have double-counted or missed any income from Column A or Column B.)*

Inventory (aka Cost of Goods Sold, COGS)

While most small businesses are required to keep inventory, there is an exception in the tax code for Independent Writers, Artists, & Performers, using NAICS code 711510.[6] If this is you, keeping inventory is optional. All others must track it. See TFH *Chapter 4, Business Expenses for more.*

Are you a retailer or nonservice business outside the category of
Independent Writers, Artists & Performers?   [YES]   [NO]

Did you have significant unsold inventory at the end of the year?   [YES]   [NO]

Inventory Calculation (Cost of Goods Sold, aka COGS)

COGS is a number that rolls over from last year's tax return to this year's. Specifically, last year's "ending inventory" number (line 41 on your Schedule C) becomes this year's beginning inventory number (line 35 on your Schedule C).[7] On your Schedule C each year, start with your beginning inventory number; then add together your (direct cost) purchases, direct labor costs, and direct materials costs; and then subtract your amount of inventory costs that remain unsold to get your ending inventory number.

Beginning Inventory (January 1)	Ending Inventory (December 31)	Purchases Made During the Tax Year
(Find this on last year's Schedule C, Part III, line 41. If this is your first year in business, your beginning inventory is zero.) *In dollars – wholesale (not retail).*	*In dollars – wholesale (not retail).*	*Tax year purchases in dollars – wholesale.*
_____	_____	_____

Note that inventory cost refers to the cost to you, not the retail value.

(continued)

Expenses

For a business deductions deep dive, see TFH *Chapter 4. Your shortest path to a no-pain audit is to follow these deduction documentation rules from the start.*

For a cheat-sheet version, download my free Visual guide to tax deductions at www.sunlighttax.com/deductionsguide *or at this QR code:*

By listing your expenses on your tax return, you assert that you've made accurate claims and have proper documentation (receipt/mileage log/cancelled check, etc.). If examined (audited) by the IRS or local taxing authority, it is your responsibility to show this documentation.

Tally your expenses for each category, and **give only totals** *for each.*

Advertising/Marketing
Include: website hosting, CRM like Mailchimp/ConvertKit, Instagram or Facebook ads, photography of products/artwork, etc.

_____

Commissions and Fees
Application fees, bank fees, affiliate commissions, etc.

_____

Contract Labor

Anyone you paid (for a business purpose) who is not your employee.

If you paid over $600 to any individual, did you issue them the
required 1099?   [YES]   [NO]

NOTE: Do not pass go until you issue the 1099s as the law requires. If you paid anyone over $600 for your business, you may be required to issue them a 1099 (by January 31). If you're late, file them ASAP, because penalties increase. For help on issuing 1099s, see the IRS instructions at https://www.irs.gov/pub/irs-pdf/i1099mec.pdf *or at this QR code:*

or take my mini-course at www.sunlighttax.com/1099 *or at this QR code:*

(continued)

Health Insurance Premiums *(if not employer-provided, and only if you were **not** offered coverage by your employer or spouse's employer)*

_____

Insurance Premiums for Your Business (other than health insurance): *i.e., business liability insurance, etc.*

_____

Legal and Accounting Fees

_____

Rent – machinery or other

_____

Rent – studio/office

_____

Repairs

_____

Supplies (include books/periodicals, and small equipment under $300)

Things that get used up within a year, like paper. Items with a useful life of several years are assets and may need to be depreciated: list those in the Assets section.[8]

_____

Taxes and Licenses

This is not for sales tax or income tax. Include business franchise taxes, as well as fees for any licenses you hold.

_____

Utilities (other than for a home office/studio): electric, gas, oil, water, etc.

Do not include phone or internet expenses (see: Office Expenses)

_____

Office Expenses

This is only for an office/studio outside of your home.

Postage/Shipping

_____

Printing

_____

Internet/Phone

For internet and phone, you may only deduct your business use percentage, which cannot be 100% if you use the same plan for personal use.[9] Multiply the first column by the percentage to get your deductible total in the third column.

Internet	× Percent business use	= allowable deduction
_____	_____	_____
Phone	× Percent business use	= allowable deduction
_____	_____	_____

(continued)

Other office expenses

_____

Asset Purchases

Assets are purchases that last longer than a year (otherwise, they're supplies). Common examples: computer, desk, etching press, table saw. Many assets that are technically depreciable may be expensed in a single year.[10] List all assets here. Never list the same item twice. If you note it here, it should not be included in your "supply" total above, and vice versa. See TFH *Chapter 4 for details on assets and depreciation.*

Did you purchase any business assets during the tax year?   [YES]   [NO]

List of business asset purchases

Description of Asset *(i.e., computer, drill press, etc.)*	Date of Purchase[11]	Purchase Price *(total, including sales tax and installation fees)*

Meals

Total expense for meals with business associates to conduct business (i.e., with clients, prospects, etc.). Client meals are never solo – you must meet with someone for a business purpose.[12]

Travel for Business

Local Travel

Expenses for local travel (taxi, ride share, public transport, etc.)		
Total annual cost of transit passes	× Percentage used for business trips excluding commute	= deductible portion of transit passes

Did you travel overnight for your business during the year?　　　[YES]　　[NO]

Travel Expenses Away from Home

See TFH Chapter 4 for details on travel deduction rules, especially the difference between domestic and international travel rules for airfare. See also this IRS explainer: https://www.irs.gov/taxtopics/tc511.

(continued)

Total Travel Expenses excluding meals (flights, hotels, taxis while away, etc.)

_____

Travel Meals (actual cost) (choose this only if larger than per diem deduction)

_____

You can either *expense the actual cost of meals* or *use the federal per diem rate by location + # of days.*[13] *Consider listing both here, and then choose the larger of the two as your deduction.*

Per diem travel (for travel meals) (choose this only if larger than the actual meals deduction)

Travel Dates for Per Diem Meals Calculation

The per diem calculation is a government-set average rate for your business meals, rather than your actual costs. See TFH *Chapter 4 for how to do the per diem calculation. Look up the per diem rates for your destination at this link for US travel, see* https://www.gsa.gov/travel/plan-book/per-diem-rates. For international *travel, see* https://allowances.state.gov/web920/per_diem.asp?.

You can also use the following QR codes to get to those URLs:

Note: Select the relevant *tax year*, not the current year.

Name of destination (city and state or city and country)	Number of days spent working at this destination

Home Office Deduction

*Must be used **exclusively** for business (i.e., not your dining room).[14] It is OK to sub-divide a larger room, but the division must be clear. If you moved during the year and had an office at more than one address, add multiple entries here.*

(continued)

Office

Total square footage of your home	Office or studio square footage
_____	_____

What date did you begin using your home office for business?

_____

Total cost of rent for your home (for the year)	Or, total mortgage interest for your home (for the year)
_____	_____

Total cost of insurance for your home (for the year)	Total cost of utilities for your home (for the year). *Exclude* the phone/internet.
_____	_____
mortgage insurance or renters' insurance	

Other costs of running your home (for the year)

that are partly applied to your studio/office

_____

Total real estate taxes (for the year)

_____

Any costs that are *only* for your home office/studio? (please list)

as in: painting, soundproofing, or special lighting for the office, etc.

These direct expenses you may take in full, *not as a percentage of your total office-to-home ratio.*

_____

_____

_____

_____

_____

_____

• Repeat these questions for a second office, if you moved during the year.

Do you use a vehicle for business purposes?   [YES]   [NO]

If yes, answer the following vehicle questions.

Vehicle Information

Business Parking and Tolls Expense	
_____	
What date did you begin using the vehicle for business purposes?	What date did you purchase the vehicle?
_____	_____

(continued)

What was the purchase price?

_____

Do you have a mileage log for the vehicle for the tax year?   [YES]   [NO]

This is the number-one most audited part of a freelancer's tax return. Be sure you keep a log, as the IRS requires you to. MileIQ is a good tracking app. QuickBooks Self-Employed has a tracking app, or a notebook in the car is fine, too.

Total miles for the year	Total commuting miles, if you tracked them
	commuting is not deductible

Total business miles

_____

Can include trips to offsite locations, client meetings, supply runs or going from a first place of work to a second place of work.

Total Actual Expenses for Your Car

Actual expenses include gas, repairs, tires, lease payments, insurance, etc. If you're taking the mileage method (which is generally better than taking the actual expense method) and have a mileage log, skip this question. If you're not sure, list both, and deduct the larger.

Total actual expenses of operating the vehicle for the year

_____

Other Expenses for Your Business

For details on what goes in each of these categories, see TFH *Chapter 4.*

Dues and Subscriptions

_____

Research

_____

Professional Development

_____

List any other business expenses here that were not asked for elsewhere.

_____

_____

_____

_____

_____

_____

_____

Feel free to describe them if you're not sure how to categorize them.

(continued)

Miscellaneous Income

List any miscellaneous income not from self-employment here, and describe (jury duty, hobby income, gambling winnings, Medical Savings Account, unemployment income, scholarships, etc.).

_____

_____

_____

_____

_____

_____

_____

This category is for income that is not *related to your business. Think of this as the "random income" section.*

Rental Income

Did you have rental income from real estate (including Airbnb, etc.)?   [YES]   [NO]
If yes, answer the following.

Your Properties

Copy this section as many times as you need to for multiple properties.

Property 1

Physical Address

_____

_____

_____

_____

_____

_____

_____

_____

What was the cost of the property?

_____

Do you know the breakdown between the cost of the house/building
versus the cost of the land?[15]   [YES]   [NO]

Cost of the house/building	Cost of the land
_____	_____
Is this your primary residence (i.e., Airbnb-style rental of your primary residence)? [YES] [NO]	

(continued)

Number of days rented during the year	Number of personal-use days during the year

Type of property	Gross rents received
• [Single-family residence] • [Multifamily residence] • [Vacation rental] • [Commercial]	

Expenses for Your Rental

Advertising	Auto and travel
Cleaning and maintenance	Commissions
Insurance	Legal and other professional fees
Management fees *(Includes Airbnb/VRBO fees)*	Mortgage interest
Other interest	Repairs

Supplies	Taxes
Utilities	Other

Personal Expenses

How much mortgage interest did you pay, if any?

_____

How much student loan interest did you pay, if any?

_____

Child Care Expenses

Did you have child care expenses during the tax year?   [YES]   [NO]

Child care expenses, including summer camp (not sleepaway), are deductible if you paid them for a dependent child under 13, or costs of caring for a disabled dependent or spouse, so you could work, look for work, or attend school.

Name of provider

_____

Address

_____

(continued)

Amount paid during tax year

_____

Federal Tax ID Number

EIN (business) or Social Security number (individual)

_____

If you have multiple children, which child does this apply to?

_____

Did you contribute to a 529 plan for education expenses?	[YES] [NO]

How much did you contribute to the 529 plan?	What is the name of the 529 plan?
_____	
_____	
_____	
_____	_____

Was your entire household covered by medical insurance
for the entire year?

If not, provide exemption(s) here: [YES]   [NO]

Medical insurance exemptions, if any

_____

Check here if you/your family did not have health insurance and did not have an exemption (i.e., you had a gap in coverage/no coverage).	[YES]	[NO]
Did you purchase health care coverage on the marketplace (healthcare.gov)? *If yes, be sure to have your form 1095A.*	[YES]	[NO]

Medical Expenses

You can deduct medical expenses only if you itemize, and they are pretty high compared to your income – typically young, healthy people can't.[16] *See* TFH *Chapter 9 for full details.*

Did you have medical expenses that exceeded 7.5% of your income?   [YES]   [NO]

If no, skip to the next section.

Specific Medical Expenses

Insurance premiums	Doctors, dentists, orthodontists
Medicine and prescriptions	Miles driven for medical care

Other Medical Expenses

Item 1

Description	Amount

(continued)

Taxes Paid

State and local income tax *(do not repeat W2 info here)*

_____

Real estate property tax

_____

Personal property tax (cars, etc.)

_____

Was this based on the value of your car (versus a flat fee)?   [YES]   [NO]

Did you make any charitable contributions for the tax year?   [YES]   [NO]

Charitable Contributions

Charitable contributions are only deductible if you itemize, *which only 10% of tax-payers do.*[17] *See* TFH *Chapter 9 for more detail.*

Note: if you donated artwork that you made, *it is probably not deductible.*

Charity Name

Charity Name	Total cash donations to charity

Total non-cash donations to charity (i.e., seven bags of clothing, one dishwasher, etc.)

_____

_____

_____

_____

_____

_____

_____

You/Your Spouse's IRA Contribution

See TFH *Chapter 14 for information on contributing to tax-advantaged retirement accounts, like a Traditional or Roth IRA.*

	You	**Spouse**
Did you make an IRA contribution this year, or do you plan to? *You have until April 15 to make a contribution that counts toward last year's taxes*	[YES] [NO] *(please say yes)*	[YES] [NO] *(please say yes)*
IRA type	• [Traditional IRA] • [Roth IRA]	• [Traditional IRA] • [Roth IRA]

(continued)

	You	**Spouse**
Amount contributed/planned *The limit for 2025 is $7,000 if under 50 and $8,000 if over 50. See updated numbers each year at* https://www .irs.gov/retirement-plans/plan-participant-employee/retirement-topics-ira-contribution-limits.	_____	_____
Date of contribution	_____	_____

Additional Nonworkplace Retirement Accounts

See TFH *Chapter 14 for information on contributing to tax-advantaged retirement accounts when you're self-employed.*

Account 1 (repeat as needed for multiple accounts)

	You	**Spouse**
Did you contribute to any other nonworkplace retirement account, or do you plan to (SEP, SIMPLE, Solo 401k)? If yes, please answer the following:	[YES] [NO]	[YES] [NO]
Type of account	_____	_____
Amount contributed	_____	_____
Date of contribution	_____	_____

Health Savings Accounts (HSAs)

	You	**Spouse**
Did you have a high-deductible health care plan last year?	[YES] [NO]	[YES] [NO]
Did you contribute to an HSA account?	_____	_____
Was the coverage for a single taxpayer or for the family?	• [INDIVIDUAL] • [FAMILY]	• [INDIVIDUAL] • [FAMILY]
HSA contribution amount	_____	_____
Date of contribution	_____	_____

Estimated Quarterly Tax Payments

This is one of the hardest parts of working for yourself. TFH *Chapter 2 covers how estimated taxes work.*

Did you pay estimated quarterly tax payments last year? *There is no automatic reporting of estimates you paid, so don't forget to report yours.*[18]

[YES]   [NO]

If yes, please list.

Your estimated tax payments:

1st quarter IRS payment amount	Date paid	1st quarter state payment amount	Date paid
_____	_____	_____	_____
2nd quarter IRS	Date paid	2nd quarter state	Date paid
_____	_____	_____	_____

(continued)

3rd quarter IRS payment	Date paid	3rd quarter state payment	Date paid
4th quarter IRS payment	Date paid	4th quarter state payment	Date paid

Your spouse's estimated tax payments:

1st quarter IRS payment amount	Date paid	1st quarter state payment amount	Date paid
2nd quarter IRS	Date paid	2nd quarter state	Date paid
3rd quarter IRS payment	Date paid	3rd quarter state payment	Date paid
4th quarter IRS payment	Date paid	4th quarter state payment	Date paid

Other Important Questions

Did you buy or sell a house last year?   [YES]   [NO]

House sale

If so, include your HUD/settlement statement in tax documents.

Sale Price	Date Sold
Original Purchase Price	Purchase Date
Did you pay or receive alimony? [YES] [NO]	If yes, please provide details.
Did you adopt a child? [YES] [NO]	If yes, please provide details.

Did you suffer a catastrophic loss (theft, natural disaster)?   [YES]   [NO]

(continued)

If yes, provide details, including any insurance reimbursements.

_____

_____

_____

_____

Was it in a federally declared disaster area?   [YES]   [NO]

Tax Documents Checklist

The following is a list of tax documents that you need, if you received them.

Remember to practice good digital security, since personally identifiable information is included in your tax documents. Genius Scan and Scannable are great apps for converting smartphone photos to PDFs.

- A copy of last year's tax return

Sources of Income Documents

- Salaries and wages (Form W2)

- Freelance income (1099-NEC, 1099-K, 1099-MISC, etc.)

- Interest (1099-INT)

- Dividends (1099-DIV) *Include the entire statement*

- Stock sales (1099-B) *Provide your cost basis if not shown on form 1099-B, and include the entire statement*

- Digital asset sales *This includes cryptocurrency, NFTs, stablecoins, etc. Ask your crypto broker to see what tax reporting is available. For every digital asset sale, you need the date purchased, payment amount, sale date, and sale value.*

- State income tax refunds

- Unemployment compensation (1099-G)

- Social Security benefits (SSA-1099)

- Pension benefits or IRA distributions (1099-R)

- Cancellation of indebtedness (1099-C)

- Documentation for miscellaneous income *Jury duty, gambling winnings, medical savings accounts, scholarships, hobbies, etc.*

- Any other official-looking documents not listed here

- Do you believe there are any state or local tax incentives that you qualify for? *Examples: The first-time DC homebuyer credit, a renter's credit, local clean energy incentive. Explain/identify which local or state tax credit you believe qualify for and why, or add this task to your Tax Questions research list.*

- Schedule K-1 if a shareholder in an S-corporation or Partnership

- Schedule K-1 for trust or estate

Health Insurance

- Form 1095-A if you received insurance on the marketplace (healthcare.gov)

- Form 1095-B or 1095-C if your health insurance was not from the marketplace

- Massachusetts residents only Form 1099-HC

Taxes Paid

- Documents to demonstrate real estate property tax payments

- Documents to demonstrate personal property tax payments (i.e., for your car)

(continued)

Miscellaneous Tax Documents

Charitable receipts are for your records, not for tax prep. If you gave over $250 to an organization, you are required to maintain a receipt/letter from that organization.

- Receipts for charitable donations of cars.

- Mortgage interest (Form 1098).

- Student loan interest (Form 1098).

- If you put money into a 529 plan, gather documentation with the 529 plan name on it.

- 1099-Q if you withdrew from a 529 plan.

- If you bought or sold a house or other real estate last year, gather the HUD/ settlement statement.

- If you made energy-efficient home improvements, gather copies of receipts (windows, solar, etc.).

- Any letters or notices you received from the IRS or state.

Foreign Bank Accounts

Did you earn any income outside the United States? [YES] [NO]	If yes, please provide details.
Did you have a bank account(s) outside the United States? [YES] [NO]	At any time during the year, did the combined total in all foreign accounts exceed $10,000? [YES] [NO]

If you answered yes to this question, complete the following questions: any time during the year, did the combined total in all foreign accounts exceed $10,000.

Bank 1 (repeat this info for each foreign bank account)

Bank Name	What was the peak value in the account last year?
Bank Location (address)	Bank Account Number

Now review those four lists you've been keeping as you worked:

- Your tax questions
- Decisions you need to make
- Action items
- Upcoming life/income changes that may require adjustments for this year

Is there anything else to note on those lists (for yourself, your records, or your accountant if you have one) that's not captured here? Are there tax concerns you'd like to address? Pick the corresponding list, and write it there.

Plan a reward. You've completed the hard part.

What's your reward for finishing this work?

Now, you're ready to do your taxes, or give this organizer to your tax preparer. If you're going DIY, see *TFH* Chapter 9 for instructions on doing the input part of your taxes.

When to Call in a Tax Pro

I hope to help you do your own taxes. But just because you can read a book by a doctor on healthy living doesn't mean you should do your own heart surgery. Sometimes taxes require expert guidance. If so, file for an extension to give yourself time, and then seek an expert.

TFH Chapter 10 covers in detail how to triage whether to DIY your taxes or get expert help. If you are low on funds, the Volunteer Income Tax Assistance (VITA) program is a good source of free help.

Figure 4.3 is a checklist to help determine if you need a pro.

Do you need a tax pro? Check all that apply:

☐ A big transition or change in financial circumstance

☐ Marriage

☐ Divorce

☐ Recent or upcoming retirement

☐ Complex household (the Volunteer Income Tax Assistance (VITA) program is a good resource for this - and it's free)

☐ Income threshold concerns (like if you'll lose your subsidized housing if you earn over a certain amount)

☐ Buying or selling real estate

☐ Buying or selling a business

☐ Large gain in income

☐ Multiple states

☐ International tax situations

☐ Complex real estate transactions

☐ Complex investments

☐ Complex depreciation/capital expenditures (like building a studio or a new home office)

☐ Inheritance

☐ Corporate tax returns (these are an S corporation, a C corporation, or a partnership. LLCs do not create a separate tax entity, so this does not apply to a solo LLC)

☐ Tax entity formation (decisions about forming any of the above: note, *TFH* Chapter 12 teaches you about this)

☐ Tax resolution issues (audits, IRS letters, back taxes, etc.)

☐ A need to make complex decisions/expert guidance

If you checked any of the above, consider hiring a tax professional for your tax return.

Figure 4.3   Do you need a tax pro?
Source: © Hannah Cole/Sunlight Tax

Notes

1. Kagan, "Filing Status: What it Means on Your Taxes, Types."
2. "Topic no. 455, Moving expenses for members of the Armed Forces," *U.S. Department of the Treasury, Internal Revenue Service*, last modified November 15, 2024, https://www.irs.gov/taxtopics/tc455.
3. "Pay taxes by Electronic Funds Withdrawal," *U.S. Department of the Treasury, Internal Revenue Service*, last modified September 27, 2024, https://www.irs.gov/payments/pay-taxes-by-electronic-funds-withdrawal.
4. "Types of payments available to individuals through Direct Pay," *U.S. Department of the Treasury, Internal Revenue Service*, last modified November 12, 2024, https://www.irs.gov/payments/types-of-payments-available-to-individuals-through-direct-pay.
5. U.S. Department of the Treasury, Internal Revenue Service. *2024 Instructions for Schedule C.* 2024, Washington, DC.
6. "Adjusted gross income defined," *Code of Federal Regulations*, title 26 (1972): § 62(a)(2)(B), https://www.law.cornell.edu/uscode/text/26/62; "Joint Committee Report JCS-10-87: General Explanation of the Tax Reform Act of 1986," *Tax Notes*, May 4, 1987, https://www.taxnotes.com/research/federal/legislative-documents/jct-blue-books/joint-committee-report-jcs-10-87-general-explanation-of-the/1r3py.
7. U.S. Department of the Treasury, Internal Revenue Service. *2024 Instructions for Schedule C.* 2024, Washington, DC, C-16.
8. There's a rule that allows you to deduct items that cost under $2,500 as a supply. It's called the de minimis safe harbor rule. Use this endnote for further reading. "Capital Expenditures; in general," *Code of Federal Regulations*, title 26 (2015): 550–558, https://www.govinfo.gov/content/pkg/CFR-2015-title26-vol4/pdf/CFR-2015-title26-vol4-part1-subjectgroup-id149.pdf. See "Tangible Property Regulations - Frequently Asked Questions," *U.S. Department of the Treasury, Internal Revenue Service*, accessed December 3, 2024, https://www.irs.gov/businesses/small-businesses-self-employed/tangible-property-final-regulations#Ademinimis; U.S. Department of the Treasury, Internal Revenue Service. *Instructions for Forms 1099-INT and 1099-OID.* 2023, Washington, DC, 1.
9. "Topic no. 509, Business use of home," *U.S. Department of the Treasury, Internal Revenue Service*, last modified September 18, 2024, https://www.irs.gov/taxtopics/tc509.
10. Using what's called a Section §179 expense. See chapter 4 of Taxes for Humans for details, or consult this: U.S. Department of the Treasury, Internal Revenue Service. *How To Depreciate Property.* 2023, Pub. 946, Washington, DC, 96.

11. If this date is different from the date you started using the asset in your business, then list the first use date instead of purchase date.

12. U.S. Department of the Treasury, Internal Revenue Service. *Travel, Gift, and Car Expenses.* 2023, Pub. 463, Washington, DC, 59.

13. *Travel, Gift, and Car Expenses*, Pub. 463, 16.

14. "2024 Instructions for Schedule C (2024)," C-11.

15. The reason for this question is that buildings are depreciable, but land is not. You therefore may not depreciate the entire property. The key to making this calculation is knowing the building cost vs. land cost breakdown. Seek professional help if this remains unclear, at least for setting up your depreciation in the first year.

16. "Topic no. 502, Medical and dental expenses," *U.S. Department of the Treasury, Internal Revenue Service*, last modified June 23, 2025, https://www.irs.gov/taxtopics/tc502.

17. See U.S. Department of the Treasury, Internal Revenue Service. Charitable Contributions. 2023, Pub. 526, 2, Washington, DC.

18. "Pay as you go, so you won't owe: A guide to withholding, estimated taxes and ways to avoid the estimated tax penalty," *U.S. Department of the Treasury, Internal Revenue Service*, lastmodifiedDecember17,2024,https://www.irs.gov/payments/pay-as-you-go-so-you-wont-owe-a-guide-to-withholding-estimated-taxes-and-ways-to-avoid-the-estimated-tax-penalty.

Part 5

Tax Review and Adjustment for Next Year

Your signature attests that you've reviewed for accuracy and consent to file your taxes. Review it *before* you sign it. Don't stick it in a drawer without looking. Reviewing your tax return ensures you:

- Catch mistakes (before they turn into an audit)
- Prevent over- or under-paying your taxes, and possibly breaking the law
- Have confidence from knowing your numbers
- Don't unknowingly tie your fate to a tax-cheating spouse[1]

You don't need to be a tax expert or even review every line. I recommend you review the first two pages of your tax return, which are the summary pages (see Figures 5.1 and 5.2).

Form **1040** Department of the Treasury—Internal Revenue Service
U.S. Individual Income Tax Return **2024** OMB No. 1545-0074 IRS Use Only—Do not write or staple in this space.

For the year Jan. 1–Dec. 31, 2024, or other tax year beginning ______, 2024, ending ______, 20 ____ See separate instructions.

Your first name and middle initial	Last name		**Your social security number**
If joint return, spouse's first name and middle initial	Last name		**Spouse's social security number**
Home address (number and street). If you have a P.O. box, see instructions.		Apt. no.	**Presidential Election Campaign** Check here if you, or your spouse if filing jointly, want $3 to go to this fund. Checking a box below will not change your tax or refund. ☐ **You** ☐ **Spouse**
City, town, or post office. If you have a foreign address, also complete spaces below.	State	ZIP code	
Foreign country name	Foreign province/state/county	Foreign postal code	

Filing Status
Check only one box.
☐ Single
☐ Married filing jointly (even if only one had income)
☐ Married filing separately (MFS)
☐ Head of household (HOH)
☐ Qualifying surviving spouse (QSS)
If you checked the MFS box, enter the name of your spouse. If you checked the HOH or QSS box, enter the child's name if the qualifying person is a child but not your dependent: ______
☐ If treating a nonresident alien or dual-status alien spouse as a U.S. resident for the entire tax year, check the box and enter their name (see instructions and attach statement if required): ______

Digital Assets At any time during 2024, did you: (a) receive (as a reward, award, or payment for property or services); or (b) sell, exchange, or otherwise dispose of a digital asset (or a financial interest in a digital asset)? (See instructions.) ☐ **Yes** ☐ **No**

Standard Deduction **Someone can claim:** ☐ You as a dependent ☐ Your spouse as a dependent
☐ Spouse itemizes on a separate return or you were a dual-status alien

Age/Blindness **You:** ☐ Were born before January 2, 1960 ☐ Are blind **Spouse:** ☐ Was born before January 2, 1960 ☐ Is blind

Dependents (see instructions):
If more than four dependents, see instructions and check here . . ☐

(1) First name Last name	(2) Social security number	(3) Relationship to you	(4) Check the box if qualifies for (see instructions): Child tax credit	Credit for other dependents
			☐	☐
			☐	☐
			☐	☐
			☐	☐

Income

Attach Form(s) W-2 here. Also attach Forms W-2G and 1099-R if tax was withheld.
If you did not get a Form W-2, see instructions.

1a	Total amount from Form(s) W-2, box 1 (see instructions)	1a	
b	Household employee wages not reported on Form(s) W-2	1b	
c	Tip income not reported on line 1a (see instructions)	1c	
d	Medicaid waiver payments not reported on Form(s) W-2 (see instructions)	1d	
e	Taxable dependent care benefits from Form 2441, line 26	1e	
f	Employer-provided adoption benefits from Form 8839, line 29	1f	
g	Wages from Form 8919, line 6	1g	
h	Other earned income (see instructions)	1h	
i	Nontaxable combat pay election (see instructions) . . . 1i		
z	Add lines 1a through 1h	1z	
2a	Tax-exempt interest . . . 2a ___ b Taxable interest	2b	
3a	Qualified dividends . . . 3a ___ b Ordinary dividends	3b	
4a	IRA distributions . . . 4a ___ b Taxable amount	4b	
5a	Pensions and annuities . . 5a ___ b Taxable amount	5b	
6a	Social security benefits . . 6a ___ b Taxable amount	6b	
c	If you elect to use the lump-sum election method, check here (see instructions) ☐		
7	Capital gain or (loss). Attach Schedule D if required. If not required, check here ☐	7	
8	Additional income from Schedule 1, line 10	8	
9	Add lines 1z, 2b, 3b, 4b, 5b, 6b, 7, and 8. This is your **total income**	9	
10	Adjustments to income from Schedule 1, line 26	10	
11	Subtract line 10 from line 9. This is your **adjusted gross income**	11	
12	**Standard deduction or itemized deductions** (from Schedule A)	12	
13	Qualified business income deduction from Form 8995 or Form 8995-A	13	
14	Add lines 12 and 13	14	
15	Subtract line 14 from line 11. If zero or less, enter -0-. This is your **taxable income**	15	

Attach Sch. B if required.

Standard Deduction for—
• Single or Married filing separately, $14,600
• Married filing jointly or Qualifying surviving spouse, $29,200
• Head of household, $21,900
• If you checked any box under *Standard Deduction*, see instructions.

For Disclosure, Privacy Act, and Paperwork Reduction Act Notice, see separate instructions. Cat. No. 11320B Form **1040** (2024)

Figure 5.1 Form 1040 page 1.
Source: https://www.irs.gov/pub/irs-pdf/f1040.pdf Public domain

Tax and Credits	16	**Tax** (see instructions). Check if any from Form(s): 1 ☐ 8814 2 ☐ 4972 3 ☐ _____		16	
	17	Amount from Schedule 2, line 3		17	
	18	Add lines 16 and 17		18	
	19	Child tax credit or credit for other dependents from Schedule 8812		19	
	20	Amount from Schedule 3, line 8		20	
	21	Add lines 19 and 20		21	
	22	Subtract line 21 from line 18. If zero or less, enter -0-		22	
	23	Other taxes, including self-employment tax, from Schedule 2, line 21		23	
	24	Add lines 22 and 23. This is your **total tax**		24	
Payments	25	Federal income tax withheld from:			
	a	Form(s) W-2	25a		
	b	Form(s) 1099	25b		
	c	Other forms (see instructions)	25c		
	d	Add lines 25a through 25c		25d	
If you have a qualifying child, attach Sch. EIC.	26	2024 estimated tax payments and amount applied from 2023 return		26	
	27	Earned income credit (EIC)	27		
	28	Additional child tax credit from Schedule 8812	28		
	29	American opportunity credit from Form 8863, line 8	29		
	30	Reserved for future use	30		
	31	Amount from Schedule 3, line 15	31		
	32	Add lines 27, 28, 29, and 31. These are your **total other payments and refundable credits**		32	
	33	Add lines 25d, 26, and 32. These are your **total payments**		33	
Refund	34	If line 33 is more than line 24, subtract line 24 from line 33. This is the amount you **overpaid**		34	
	35a	Amount of line 34 you want **refunded to you**. If Form 8888 is attached, check here ☐		35a	
Direct deposit? See instructions.	b	Routing number _____ c Type: ☐ Checking ☐ Savings			
	d	Account number _____			
	36	Amount of line 34 you want **applied to your 2025 estimated tax**	36		
Amount You Owe	37	Subtract line 33 from line 24. This is the **amount you owe.** For details on how to pay, go to *www.irs.gov/Payments* or see instructions		37	
	38	Estimated tax penalty (see instructions)	38		

Third Party Designee

Do you want to allow another person to discuss this return with the IRS? See instructions . . . . ☐ **Yes.** Complete below. ☐ **No**

Designee's name		Phone no.		Personal identification number (PIN)	

Sign Here

Under penalties of perjury, I declare that I have examined this return and accompanying schedules and statements, and to the best of my knowledge and belief, they are true, correct, and complete. Declaration of preparer (other than taxpayer) is based on all information of which preparer has any knowledge.

Your signature	Date	Your occupation	If the IRS sent you an Identity Protection PIN, enter it here (see inst.)

Joint return? See instructions. Keep a copy for your records.

Spouse's signature. If a joint return, **both** must sign.	Date	Spouse's occupation	If the IRS sent your spouse an Identity Protection PIN, enter it here (see inst.)

Phone no.	Email address

Paid Preparer Use Only

Preparer's name	Preparer's signature	Date	PTIN	Check if: ☐ Self-employed
Firm's name			Phone no.	
Firm's address			Firm's EIN	

Go to *www.irs.gov/Form1040* for instructions and the latest information.   Form **1040** (2024)

Figure 5.2   Form 1040 page 2.

Source: https://www.irs.gov/pub/irs-pdf/f1040.pdf Public domain

Then review your Schedule C (Figures 5.3 and 5.4).

SCHEDULE C (Form 1040)

Department of the Treasury
Internal Revenue Service

Profit or Loss From Business
(Sole Proprietorship)

Attach to Form 1040, 1040-SR, 1040-SS, 1040-NR, or 1041; partnerships must generally file Form 1065.
Go to *www.irs.gov/ScheduleC* for instructions and the latest information.

OMB No. 1545-0074

2024

Attachment
Sequence No. **09**

Name of proprietor

Social security number (SSN)

A Principal business or profession, including product or service (see instructions)

B Enter code from instructions

C Business name. If no separate business name, leave blank.

D Employer ID number (EIN) (see instr.)

E Business address (including suite or room no.)
City, town or post office, state, and ZIP code

F Accounting method: **(1)** ☐ Cash **(2)** ☐ Accrual **(3)** ☐ Other (specify)

G Did you "materially participate" in the operation of this business during 2024? If "No," see instructions for limit on losses   ☐ Yes ☐ No

H If you started or acquired this business during 2024, check here   ☐

I Did you make any payments in 2024 that would require you to file Form(s) 1099? See instructions   ☐ Yes ☐ No

J If "Yes," did you or will you file required Form(s) 1099?   ☐ Yes ☐ No

Part I   Income

1	Gross receipts or sales. See instructions for line 1 and check the box if this income was reported to you on Form W-2 and the "Statutory employee" box on that form was checked ☐	1
2	Returns and allowances	2
3	Subtract line 2 from line 1	3
4	Cost of goods sold (from line 42)	4
5	**Gross profit.** Subtract line 4 from line 3	5
6	Other income, including federal and state gasoline or fuel tax credit or refund (see instructions)	6
7	**Gross income.** Add lines 5 and 6	7

Part II   Expenses. Enter expenses for business use of your home **only** on line 30.

8	Advertising	8	18	Office expense (see instructions)	18
9	Car and truck expenses (see instructions)	9	19	Pension and profit-sharing plans	19
10	Commissions and fees	10	20	Rent or lease (see instructions):	
11	Contract labor (see instructions)	11	a	Vehicles, machinery, and equipment	20a
12	Depletion	12	b	Other business property	20b
13	Depreciation and section 179 expense deduction (not included in Part III) (see instructions)	13	21	Repairs and maintenance	21
			22	Supplies (not included in Part III)	22
			23	Taxes and licenses	23
			24	Travel and meals:	
14	Employee benefit programs (other than on line 19)	14	a	Travel	24a
15	Insurance (other than health)	15	b	Deductible meals (see instructions)	24b
16	Interest (see instructions):		25	Utilities	25
a	Mortgage (paid to banks, etc.)	16a	26	Wages (less employment credits)	26
b	Other	16b	27a	Other expenses (from line 48)	27a
17	Legal and professional services	17	b	Energy efficient commercial bldgs deduction (attach Form 7205)	27b

28	**Total expenses** before expenses for business use of home. Add lines 8 through 27b	28
29	Tentative profit or (loss). Subtract line 28 from line 7	29
30	Expenses for business use of your home. Do not report these expenses elsewhere. Attach Form 8829 unless using the simplified method. See instructions. **Simplified method filers only:** Enter the total square footage of (a) your home: _____ and (b) the part of your home used for business: _____ . Use the Simplified Method Worksheet in the instructions to figure the amount to enter on line 30	30
31	**Net profit or (loss).** Subtract line 30 from line 29. • If a profit, enter on both **Schedule 1 (Form 1040), line 3,** and on **Schedule SE, line 2.** (If you checked the box on line 1, see instructions.) Estates and trusts, enter on **Form 1041, line 3.** • If a loss, you **must** go to line 32.	31
32	If you have a loss, check the box that describes your investment in this activity. See instructions. • If you checked 32a, enter the loss on both **Schedule 1 (Form 1040), line 3,** and on **Schedule SE, line 2.** (If you checked the box on line 1, see the line 31 instructions.) Estates and trusts, enter on **Form 1041, line 3.** • If you checked 32b, you **must** attach Form 6198. Your loss may be limited.	32a ☐ All investment is at risk. 32b ☐ Some investment is not at risk.

For Paperwork Reduction Act Notice, see the separate instructions.   Cat. No. 11334P   Schedule C (Form 1040) 2024

Figure 5.3   Schedule C page 1.

Taxes for Humans

Part III   Cost of Goods Sold (see instructions)

33   Method(s) used to value closing inventory: **a** ☐ Cost   **b** ☐ Lower of cost or market   **c** ☐ Other (attach explanation)

34   Was there any change in determining quantities, costs, or valuations between opening and closing inventory? If "Yes," attach explanation . . . . ☐ Yes   ☐ No

35   Inventory at beginning of year. If different from last year's closing inventory, attach explanation . . . | 35 |

36   Purchases less cost of items withdrawn for personal use . . . . | 36 |

37   Cost of labor. Do not include any amounts paid to yourself . . . . | 37 |

38   Materials and supplies . . . . | 38 |

39   Other costs . . . . | 39 |

40   Add lines 35 through 39 . . . . | 40 |

41   Inventory at end of year . . . . | 41 |

42   **Cost of goods sold.** Subtract line 41 from line 40. Enter the result here and on line 4 . . . . . | 42 |

Part IV   Information on Your Vehicle. Complete this part **only** if you are claiming car or truck expenses on line 9 and are not required to file Form 4562 for this business. See the instructions for line 13 to find out if you must file Form 4562.

43   When did you place your vehicle in service for business purposes? (month/day/year)   /   /

44   Of the total number of miles you drove your vehicle during 2024, enter the number of miles you used your vehicle for:

   a   Business _____   **b** Commuting (see instructions) _____   **c** Other _____

45   Was your vehicle available for personal use during off-duty hours? . . . . ☐ Yes   ☐ No

46   Do you (or your spouse) have another vehicle available for personal use? . . . . ☐ Yes   ☐ No

47a   Do you have evidence to support your deduction? . . . . ☐ Yes   ☐ No

   b   If "Yes," is the evidence written? . . . . ☐ Yes   ☐ No

Part V   Other Expenses. List below business expenses not included on lines 8–26, line 27b, or line 30.

---	

48   **Total other expenses.** Enter here and on line 27a . . . . | 48 |

Figure 5.4   Schedule C page 2.

Source: https://www.irs.gov/pub/irs-pdf/f1040sc.pdf. Public domain

Tax Review and Adjustment for Next Year

Figures 5.5, 5.6, and 5.7 are a tax review checklist for you.

Tax review checklist

TFH Chapter 11 outlines how to do a full review.
Here's a short checklist version:

ID Info:

☐ Check the ID info. Are all the legal names, Social Security numbers (or ITINs), and addresses correct?

Income section (bottom half of page 1).
Check these to make sure they are correct.

☐ Your total income, on line 9

☐ Your adjusted gross income (AGI), (important for a lot of tax calculations) line 11

☐ Your taxable income, line 15

☐ Line 12 tells you if you itemize or take the standard deduction. This is key info to know.

Taxes (top of page 2):

☐ Line 24 tells you your total tax for the tax year. It's also a number you can refer to as you pay this year's estimated taxes.

Payments (below Taxes, on page 2):

☐ Line 25a: your W2 withholding for the year

☐ Line 26: reports your estimated tax payments for the year. If you paid estimated taxes last year, but see that this line is blank, you forgot to report them, and you must report them to get the credit (and reduced tax bill) that you deserve.

☐ Line 33: your total tax payments for the year. Your goal is for this number to be as close as possible to Line 24, your tax for the year (make sense?).

Figure 5.5 Tax review Checklist 1.

Refund:

- [ ] <u>Line 34:</u> Amount you overpaid.

- [ ] <u>Line 35a:</u> The amount of your overpayment you want refunded

- [ ] <u>Line 36:</u> Amount of your refund you want to apply to next year's estimates

Amount You Owe:

- [ ] <u>Line 37:</u> Amount of your tax underpayment, aka, the amount you owe by April 15.

- [ ] <u>Line 38:</u> estimated tax penalty, if you were supposed to pay estimates last year, but didn't (or did, but paid less than the safe harbor thresholds)

Review your Schedule C: We're leaving the summary briefly. Find your Schedule C, deeper inside your tax return.

This is the reporting for your self-employment (aka small business or freelance income). Check these numbers for accuracy:

Income:

- [ ] <u>Part I, line 1:</u> gross receipts or sales. This should accurately reflect your total income from self-employment.

Expenses:

- [ ] <u>Line 28:</u> total expenses. This number may vary from the total expenses in your books, because of special tax rules.

- [ ] Check through all the expense categories in <u>Part II</u> to make sure you listed all your deductions correctly and didn't miss any. Check this part against last year's tax return to spot missed deductions.

Figure 5.6 Tax review Checklist 2.

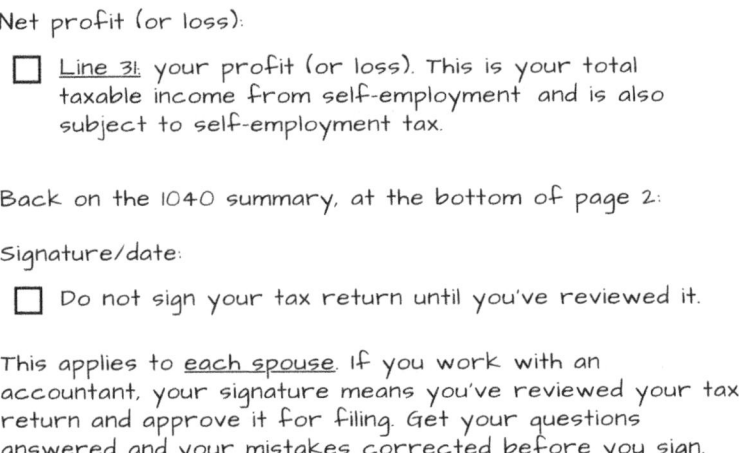

Net profit (or loss):

☐ <u>Line 31:</u> your profit (or loss). This is your total taxable income from self-employment and is also subject to self-employment tax.

Back on the 1040 summary, at the bottom of page 2:

Signature/date:

☐ Do not sign your tax return until you've reviewed it.

This applies to <u>each spouse</u>. If you work with an accountant, your signature means you've reviewed your tax return and approve it for filing. Get your questions answered and your mistakes corrected before you sign.

Figure 5.7 Tax review Checklist 3.
Source: © Hannah Cole/Sunlight Tax

Don't skip this – it matters that you *understand* what's going on. Figure 5.8 helps explain how these summary lines fit together to summarize the income you made for the prior year, the taxes you paid throughout the year, and what's left over (a refund/a tax bill).

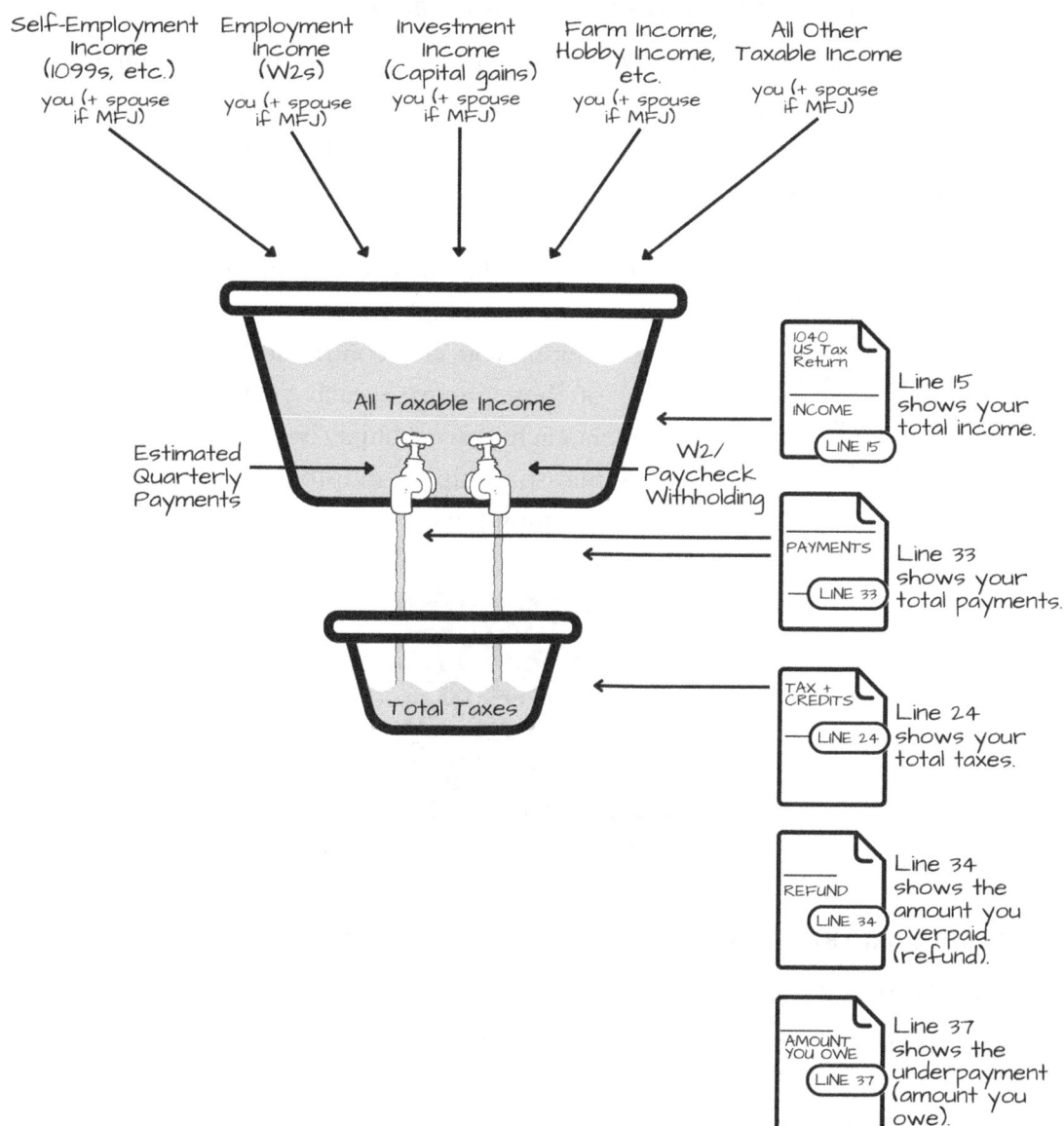

Figure 5.8 Tax buckets with 1040 lines.
Source: © Hannah Cole/Sunlight Tax

Tax Review and Adjustment for Next Year

Good job! Once you've reviewed everything and have no more questions, you're done. Time to file that bad boy.

Your Freedom Fund: Strengthen Your Savings Muscle

Let's set up your freedom fund. *TFH* Chapter 14 teaches you how to compare and choose tax-advantaged accounts. The quick and dirty version is that these accounts save you money on taxes (either in the current year or when you withdraw the funds) and boost your ability to save money.

Think of this as your path off the hustle bus. This is how you make your *money* work for you, rather than your *body*.

These are the most common tax-smart accounts available to self-employed people and the approximate amount you can contribute to them each year (most of these increase each year; see the updated numbers each year at https://www.irs.gov/retirement-plans/plan-participant-employee/retirement-topics-ira-contribution-limits).

1. **Traditional IRA:** In 2025, $7,000 if under 50 and $8,000 if over 50.

2. **Roth IRA:** In 2025, $7,000 if under 50 and $8,000 if over 50.

3. **SEP IRA:** 20% of your Schedule C *profit* (this remains the same every year).

4. **Solo 401k (a great choice, but not recommended until you run payroll):** In 2025, $23,000 if under 50 and $31,000 if over 50. See current year updated limits at https://www.irs.gov/retirement-plans/plan-participant-employee/retirement-topics-401k-and-profit-sharing-plan-contribution-limits.

Roth, Traditional, and SEP IRAs are all flexible and simple to open. You can decide each year which type is best for your circumstances that year – you're not stuck with one account for life. You can have multiple, and you can contribute to whichever one benefits you most *this year*.

Review the account types and write down which you think benefits you the most this year (read *TFH* Chapter 14 for help or research online):

_____

_____

Next, decide how much you want to contribute this year. Factors to consider: most financial experts recommend saving 10–20% of your income, with about 15% going toward retirement savings.

Line 9 on page 1 of your taxes lists your total income from last year. Multiply that by .10 or .20 to see what 10–20% of your income is: _____

BONUS: If your income on page 1, **line 11**, of your tax return is less than $38,250[2] if single, or less than $76,500 MFJ, you get an additional boost from the Retirement Saver's tax credit when you contribute. See current year amounts and details at https://www.irs.gov/retirement-plans/plan-participant-employee/retirement-savings-contributions-credit-savers-credit.

Remember, any savings is good, so pick the largest amount that feels doable. Write that here: _____

_____

If you can't save what you want this year, make a target for *next* year. Take the current year IRA maximum and calculate what weekly savings goal gets you there. If that's not doable, consider what is, and keep checking back in.

Write down your target retirement savings goal for next year: _____

Divide that by 52, for your weekly savings goal: _____

Next, open the account. Pick a brokerage (I like Vanguard or Fidelity), and call them to open the account. Move your contribution into this account. This all takes about 15 minutes.

You're not quite done. You need to invest the money in the account. This may feel intimidating, but it's important. To start, you can choose a simple mix of low-cost index funds.[3] Basic investing is not as hard as it looks. Read one good book on it, and you'll know everything you need to get started. I recommend any book by Suze Orman or Ramit Sethi. In my program Money Bootcamp, I teach a one-hour primer on investing. Find it at www.sunlighttax.com/moneybootcampimpact or use this QR code:

My final word on saving:

- Open the account, even if you don't have money now.

- Set a calendar alarm every three to six months to check your savings goal. If your financial situation changes, reviewing this goal helps you keep it prioritized and increase when possible.

- It's easier to increase the amount of savings you put into an account that's already set up than to start from no account. Opening the account helps lower the barrier to you saving when money is available.

- Use the financial freedom checklist in Figure 5.9, even if you don't have money.

Mindset moment: Building savings is like working out. Results happen over time.

Financial freedom checklist,
(even if you don't have money)

☐ Open an IRA

☐ Put something in it (anything!)

☐ Invest that money (yes, while it stays in the IRA)

☐ Put on your calendar: 3-6 month reminder to
revisit your savings amount/goals

☐ Repeat yearly

Figure 5.9 Financial freedom checklist.
Source: © Hannah Cole/Sunlight Tax

Notes

1. This is critical. If you file a Married Filing Joint tax return, you're each individually responsible for 100% of what's on it, not 50%. I have a great chapter in *TFH* if you *are* in this boat: *TFH* Chapter 20, which covers what to do if you accidentally marry a con artist.
2. This is current at the time of writing but increases each year.
3. This is not investment advice. You need to do your own research.

Part 6

Recap, Reflect, and Repeat

P hew! That was a lot of work, and having gotten this far, you deserve kudos. You just faced the hard stuff.

How will you celebrate?

_____

_____

To recap, we covered mindset issues, from fear of taxes, to foregrounding the impact you want to have in the world (through your work, community, loved ones, and yourself). We got clear on why your tax return exists: to reconcile the estimated payments you make all year with the actual totals once the year ends. We instituted three tax systems: receipts, tax documents, and bookkeeping. Receipts and tax documents need a home, which is easy to establish. Bookkeeping, on the other hand, is an ongoing job that must be finished by tax time. The work you put in during the year is work you spare yourself at tax time. Gathering your bookkeeping numbers and your tax organizer questions are the heavy lift of tax season. Reviewing your tax return before you sign it is the key to catching mistakes and knowing how close your during-the-year tax payments came to covering your total due. Reviewing helps you anticipate changes and adjust for the next tax year. And checking on your savings goals (especially in tax-advantaged accounts) is a habit that you can strengthen over time for financial stability and power.

What are your biggest learnings from working through this workbook?

_____

_____

_____

_____

What's possible now that you have more tax freedom and confidence?

_____

_____

_____

_____

Taxes Are a Fitness Routine, Not One Workout

The good and bad news of taxes is that they happen every year. You get lots of practice, and building good systems and routine will serve you *every* year. Not building good systems will cause you pain – repeatedly. It's up to you.

Facing your tax fears is the hardest part of this work, and you've done that. Setting up your systems and then creating a gentle rhythm of check-ins strengthens you for life. Here's a checklist to reinforce what you've learned and support the habit of financial growth. Rather than goodbye, I'll say congratulations on your first (and hardest!) pass, and I'll see you at this checklist (Figure 6.1) next year.

Yearly Checklist

Once per quarter:

- ☐ Do your bookkeeping
- ☐ Pay your estimated taxes
- ☐ Review your savings goals/freedom budget and emergency fund

Once per year:

- ☐ Set up receipts/tax files for next year, photograph home office & odometer (January)

- ☐ Evaluate budget. Can you increase your savings?

- ☐ Review tax return
  - How closely do your total payments (<u>page 2 line 33</u>) match your total tax (<u>page 2 line 24</u>)? How can you adjust for next year?

- ☐ Evaluate income changes, make payment adjustments for upcoming tax year (file new W4 for your employment or change estimated quarterly tax payments)

End of year:

- ☐ Finish bookkeeping near December 1

- ☐ Evaluate income, do tax planning (see *TFH* Chapter 15)

- ☐ Open or fund an IRA/other tax-smart accounts, budget for savings goals

- ☐ Plan tasks for this week/month/year
  - Add tasks to my calendar

- ☐ Reflect on the questions below

Figure 6.1 Yearly checklist.

Source: © Hannah Cole/Sunlight Tax

Annual Reflections

- How have I grown in my tax/financial work this year?

_____

_____

- What growth do I want to achieve this year?

_____

_____

- What steps will get me there?

_____

_____

- What tools will help me get there (*TFH*, this workbook, my systems, support network, etc.)?

_____

_____

- How will I celebrate this year's growth?

_____

_____

_____

Acknowledgments

Thanks to my agent, Maeve MacLysaght, for early workbook visioning; Nabilah Nathani for citations; and Mark de Leon for endless diagram revisions. Thanks to the Wiley team, for making this workbook possible. And special thanks to Annie Norbeck for editing.

About the Author

Hannah Cole is a tax expert who specializes in working with creative businesses and mission-driven solopreneurs. A long-time working artist herself (represented by the Tracey Morgan Gallery in Asheville, North Carolina), she's helped tens of thousands of self-employed people skill up with accessible tax and money education through her Money Bootcamp program, via tax workshops and speaking engagements from Florida to Alaska, and on the *Sunlight Tax* podcast. She has some fancy degrees (BA in the history of art, Yale University, and MFA in painting, Boston University) and a tax license (she's an Enrolled Agent). But what she cares about most is building community and democracy through helping badass people like you do more of your amazing work. She founded her company, Sunlight Tax, with the mission to serve visionary people who are self-employed with relevant tax and financial education so they can bring their unique vision to the world.

You can find her work at www.sunlighttax.com and all the resources mentioned in this book at www.sunlighttax.com/taxesforhumansworkbook.

YouTube: @sunlighttax

Instagram: @sunlighttax

Index

Page numbers followed by *f* and *n* refer to figures and notes, respectively.

Printed and bound by CPI Group (UK) Ltd, Croydon, CR0 4YY

07/12/2025

14785980-0001